THE WAYSIDE GARDENS COLLECTION

The DRY GARDEN

THE WAYSIDE GARDENS COLLECTION

The DRY GARDEN

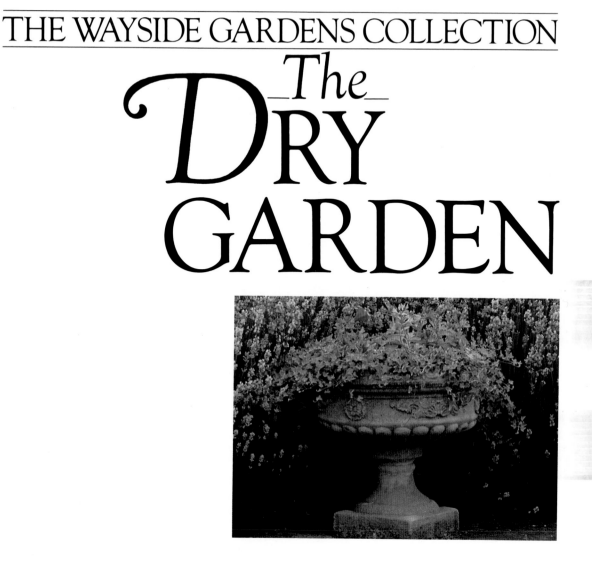

A Practical Guide to Planning & Planting

Mark Rumary

John E. Elsley, General Editor for The Wayside Gardens Collection

Sterling Publishing Co., Inc.   New York

Library of Congress Cataloguing-in-Publication Data

Rumary, Mark.
    The dry garden : a practical guide to planning & planting / Mark
Rumary.
        p. cm. — (The Wayside Gardens collection)
    Includes index.
    ISBN 0-8069-3831-5
    1. Xeriscaping. I. Title. II. Series.
SB439.8.R85 1995
635.9'5–dc20
                                                    95-18312
                                                    CIP

2 4 6 8 10 9 7 5 3 1

Published 1995 by Sterling Publishing Company, Inc.
387 Park Avenue South, New York, N.Y. 10016

The Wayside Gardens Collection edition

© 1995 Conran Octopus Limited
The original edition first published
in Great Britain by Conran Octopus Limited
37 Shelton Street, London WC2H 9HN
Text and original planting schemes © 1994 Mark Rumary
Design and layout © 1994 Conran Octopus Limited
Distributed in Canada by Sterling Publishing
%o Canadian Manda Group, One Atlantic Avenue, Suite 105
Toronto, Ontario, Canada M6K 3E7
Printed and bound in Hong Kong
All Rights Reserved

American Project Editor	Hannah Steinmetz
Project Editor	Jane O'Shea
Project Art Editor	Ann Burnham
Editors	Helen Ridge
	Caroline Davison
Designer	Lesley Craig
Picture Researcher	Helen Fickling
Production	Clare Blackwell
Illustrators	Jeremy Ford
	Vanessa Luff
	Valerie Price

Sterling ISBN 0-8069-3831-5

FRONT JACKET *Cistus × cyprius.*

BACK JACKET A dry garden planted with roses,
valerian, poppies and *Acanthus mollis* with shade
provided by *Wisteria, Campsis* and climbing roses.

PAGE 1 A border of the double poppy *Papaver*
'Fireball,' yellow Iceland poppy *(P. nudicaule)* and
Aquilegia canadensis.

PAGE 2 In this dry garden, designed by the author,
Lavandula angustifolia 'Hidcote Pink' provides a
foreground for the tall pink *Lavatera olbia* 'Rosea,'
purple *Salvia nemorosa* 'Lubecca,' *Rosa* 'Penelope'
and *Philadelphus* 'Beauclerk.' The daisy-shaped
flowers are those of *Erigeron* 'Dunkelste Aller.'

RIGHT Nasturtiums, crimson dahlias, scarlet *Salvia
microphylla neurepia* and blue *Agapanthus* fill the
border on the left of the path while *Verbena
bonariensis* grows to the right.

CONTENTS

THE PLEASURES OF
A DRY GARDEN

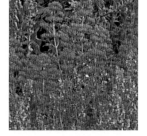

The familiar image of the gardener pottering among his plants, watering can in hand, while a sprinkler plays for hours on end in the center of a large expanse of velvety green lawn, is no longer a practical reality for many gardeners, whether because of climate, soil, legal restrictions, cost or conscience. Fortunately, however, this does not necessarily spell despair and doom.

A cool, dry garden in midsummer with mauve Nepeta, red and white valerians (Centranthus), the ferny hummocks of Dicentra formosa, foxgloves (Digitalis) and toward the rear the yellow foliage of Robinia pseudoacacia 'Frisia.' Facing the low, dry stone wall Thymus serpyllum makes a purple rug. None of the plants here is rare or difficult to grow but together they add up to a most satisfying picture.

Suitable plants for the dry garden come from a variety of habitats. As well as cladding the thin, damp peaty covering of British upland, ling or Scotch heather (Calluna vulgaris) also inhabits dry, acid, sandy soils.

Despite increased awareness of water being a precious resource, we should still be able to enjoy gardens that are an oasis of tranquility and color; what will have to change is our approach to garden design, our choice of plants and the gardening techniques. The silver lining on this cloud-free horizon is that the dry garden will be a low-maintenance garden, giving us more time to enjoy the fruits of our labors. As a garden designer, my aim is to make the best possible use of what a garden offers in the way of site and situation, climate and soil, while ensuring that it suits the taste and requirements of the client. The garden can be a place in which to entertain and a safe haven for children. It can provide beauty and color to uplift the spirits, a peaceful corner in which to escape for contemplation and an ever-changing seasonal picture. There is no reason why owners of dry gardens must lose all these delights because the heavens will not favor them.

The aim of this book is to provide a guide to the basic principles of good garden-making with allowances and alternatives included to enable us to cope with light soils, low rainfall and water restrictions.

Water: an increasingly scarce resource

Many parts of the world receive enough rain for every human and plant need, and at times far too much, while others are so short of water that barren desert is the result. Between these two extremes there are infinite variations in the level of rainfall. My garden in eastern England has a sandy soil, through which water disappears as through a sieve, and an average annual rainfall of only 21 in. As a result, I consider my garden to be extremely dry, but at least the rain is usually spread fairly evenly throughout the year and the average maximum daily temperature of the warmest month is only 72° F. Someone living in the American Southwest, with only half this amount of

The author, Mark Rumary, who has created a most delightful garden on the dry, sandy soil of Suffolk, in southeastern England.

Desert plants, like this Joshua tree (Yucca brevifolia), a native of the Mojave Desert in the U.S., must tolerate long periods without water. Most of them are unsuitable for damper, colder regions, although there are exceptions as some deserts can be very cold as well as searingly hot.

rain and months of sunshine, would doubtless find my garden decidedly damp.

Dryness in a garden, therefore, is relative but the result is the same: either we must grow only plants that are naturally adapted to the vagaries of climate and soil or we must take measures which will allow us to grow a much wider range of plants. In lands with a Mediterranean climate, such as southern California where all the rain falls in autumn and winter, the native plants rest during the hottest part of the year. As a result, gardeners in these countries must water their plants to obtain flowers in summer. In desert and semi-arid regions, gardening is imposs-ible without irrigation.

Most of northern Europe, the eastern half of the U.S. and parts of Australia have a temperate climate and are blessed (or cursed, depending on one's point of view) with more than adequate rain for much of the year. Yet these countries still have three or four months in summer when dry spells can occur, with the result that lawn grasses turn brown and other plants are put under stress. In addition, much of Europe has had two decades of below-average rainfall while many regions of North America and Africa have suffered from fierce droughts in recent years. It would appear that we may be facing a shift in climatic conditions, with scientists delivering fre-quent warnings on the possibly disastrous effects of global warming on the environment.

No one is likely to object to the unrestricted use of water in the private garden as long as there is sufficient water for more important needs. However, as demand for water increases while levels of rainfall become more erratic, even in parts of the world hitherto unused to shortages, watering has now become something of a luxury and the wise gardener should ensure that his plants can survive, when necessary, on a very limited amount of water.

9

ABOVE *Many plants with aromatic foliage, including most of our popular herbs, come from hot, dry regions. These borders incorporate the delicate foliage of purple fennel (Foeniculum vulgare 'Purpureum'), Phlomis fruticosa with yellow hooded flowers, rue (Ruta), sage (Salvia lavandulifolia) and deliciously flavored tarragon (Artemisia dracunculus). The ornamental mint (Mentha suaveolens 'Variegata') needs a rich, moist soil.*

What makes a dry garden?

Plants cannot live without water—indeed it makes up about four-fifths of their weight—but it is not only the amount of rainfall that affects how much moisture they obtain. Rapid drainage and a plant's position in the garden also affect its ability to thrive. Dry shade produced by trees, hedges and buildings is a common problem. The soil under a dense canopy of large trees, for example, with their hungry and thirsty roots, is certain to be much drier and poorer than the rest of the garden, while the soil on the shady side of a building will be cooler but also drier if the building blocks moisture-bearing winds. In fact, every garden has several microclimates that the gardener must take into consideration when planning a garden (see page 18).

Gardens which are exposed are also much more likely to suffer from drought, particularly in areas subject to drying winds. Cold, moistureless winds in spring or early summer are especially damaging.

They may dry out soils after winter rains and cause young leaves to dehydrate and blacken as the plants' roots are unable to replace the lost moisture. My own garden, with its acidic, sandy soil, is fortunately protected from drying winds by high walls, but these same walls soak up water as a lamp wick soaks up oil. In winter they cast long shadows, while in summer the shadows shorten, allowing the sun to turn the soil to dust. The effect of walls on the surrounding soil will be considered in the chapter "Designing the dry garden" (see page 15).

Making the most of a dry garden

In some countries, prolonged drought conditions may affect the gardeners' choice of style, but in most cases only the working methods have to change. The traditional way of coping with the dry garden is to water and this is essential at certain times and in specific circumstances, such as immediately after planting, on roof gardens and in very arid regions.

The first to suffer from a lack of rain are newly planted trees, shrubs and plants. "Newly," in this context, means within two years of planting in the case of trees, and within two weeks for most bedding plants. Other subjects which will soon need a very thorough watering, particularly if they are exposed to sun and wind, are shrubs and hardy plants that have shallow rooting systems such as rhododendrons, hydrangeas, phlox and Michaelmas daisies *(Aster)*; also bedding plants, such as *Impatiens* and lobelia, and leafy vegetables like tomatoes, peas, beans and marrows.

But water is becoming an increasingly scarce resource. It is beneficial, therefore, to draw upon the expertize of gardeners from around the world for whom low rainfall and periods of prolonged drought are not unusual. In Mediterranean countries, for example, where rainfall is confined to the winter months, many homes have large underground cisterns in which rainwater is collected from roofs and courtyards and stored for use during the hot and dry summer months.

In the drought-prone state of Colorado in the United States, where an estimated 40 percent of domestic water is used on the garden, a means of water conservation through creative landscaping called "xeriscaping" has been developed by the Denver Water Department. The word "xeriscape" is compiled from two words: *xeros*, the Greek word for dry, and the second half of the word landscape. The principles of this approach to garden-making are zoning, which is discussed on page 31; appropriate planning (see pages 15–31); soil improvement (see pages 33–45); efficient irrigation (see pages 46–51); the use of ground-covering mulches, such as well-rotted manure or compost, leaf mold and bark, to reduce evaporation (see page 41); suitable maintenance techniques (see page 44); and careful plant selection (see pages 53–97). The aim is to have a beautiful garden that is not a thirsty one. Although these measures may sound like a lot of hard work and expense, they will encourage strong, healthy plant growth, reduce the amount of time and resources spent on watering and cut down on weeding.

RIGHT *In this small city garden, a lawn has been dispensed with in favor of gravel and most of the flowering plants are grown in pots. The central bed with its armillary sundial is edged with ivy which can survive on a meager diet.*

RIGHT *A lesson in successful plant groupings can be learned from this arrangement in Beth Chatto's garden in Essex in south eastern England. The golden spires of foxtail lily (Eremurus Shelford hybrids) harmonize in color with the plate-like heads of Achillea 'Moonshine' and expanding seed heads of Cortaderia richardii, as well as providing strong contrast of form.*

FAR RIGHT *In dry regions it is traditional to grow flowers in containers on terraces and balconies and in courtyards. This ensures that every drop of precious water will reach the roots of the plants that need it most and none is wasted, especially if the pots are provided with saucers. Outstanding among the many plants used here is* Abutilon vitifolium album *with large white flowers and the kumquat (Fortunella japonica) with its orange fruits. The walls are clothed with the climbing rose 'Madame Grégoire Staechelin' and* Passiflora manicata.

Many of these principles can be applied successfully in other parts of the world and they were stressed by Beth Chatto in her seminal book *The Dry Garden* (published in 1978). She does not hold with watering; her plants, once established, have to cope with whatever heaven sends. To avoid having to water and to promote healthy growth, she incorporates plenty of compost or manure into the soil and then puts in "only those plants that will put up with low rainfall and complete exposure to sun and wind." However, not all of us have Beth Chatto's willpower, and very few her knowledge of plants, so that when faced with a heat wave, we are soon reaching for a watering can or hose.

Careful plant selection is vital in the dry garden. The plants described in this book come from around the world, and will not only survive, but actually enjoy dry conditions. Some come from lands with harsher climates than Britain's, such as bearberry *(Arctostaphylas)* from cold northern forests. Others like *Alyssum* and soapwort *(Saponaria)* inhabit rocky

slopes while *rugosa* roses and Californian tree poppies *(Romneya)* come from windswept sand dunes. Many plants, including *Santolina*, *Cistus* and *Osteospermum*, come from warmer climes. A few are attractive natives such as sea buckthorn *(Hippophae)* and brooms *(Cytisus)* which have naturally adapted to the driest of Britain's habitats. All plants for the dry garden should have a proven track record of thriving with little moisture for at least a good part of the year.

Most of the plants in my own garden have been chosen because they can survive many weeks without rain, but a few, allowed in because they are particular favorites, or because I feel they especially suit the style and character of the garden, have to be watered when we suffer a protracted drought. As a result, nearly all these plants, including deciduous azaleas, hydrangeas, hostas, clematis, some viburnums and fuchsias, are grouped together on the shady side of the garden so that watering need not be too frequent —it would seem that I have been subconsciously practicing zoning in my garden. If, in the future, it becomes desirable to economize still further on the use of water, either due to quirks of nature, increased water charges or the introduction of a system of water-metering, then my assembly of water "hogs" will be banished. Their removal will certainly not spoil the garden's overall effect for I know, from the remainder of the garden, that a dry garden can also be a very beautiful one.

Gardeners, like farmers, never cease to complain about their lot. Romantics may see gardening in terms of man working in harmony with nature but the reality—frosts, fierce winds, savage winters, intractable soils, false springs—is that it is a very turbulent marriage. Even though you may be struggling to cope with severe drought conditions, a dry garden has endless possibilities and potential. Whether your preference is for a formal, cottagey, romantic or contemporary setting, and whether you have rolling acres or a tiny back yard to transform, the joy of gardening is that you can create your own personal Elysium. The dry garden is only a working label—it can become whatever you want it to.

DESIGNING THE
DRY GARDEN

For any garden to be beautiful and function properly some basic design is desirable, but it is essential where the site has an inherent problem such as a lack of moisture. Careful thought and planning right at the outset will do more than anything else to minimize the risk of subsequent disappointment, to say nothing of saving time in the long run and unnecessary expense.

This Mediterranean garden, with its skillful manipulation of space, its effective use of sunshine and shadow, the sculptural forms of clipped box and the contrast between the horizontal lines of the ivy-clad walls and the upright cypress (Cupressus), shows what can be achieved with careful planning, even on a dry stony hillside. In a cooler climate, Salvia interrupta, rather than the tender Echium, could be planted next to the pinky white daisies of Erigeron karvinskianus, or the Erysimum 'Bowles' Mauve' could be repeated.

Assessing existing features

French windows open onto a sheltered patio which is separated from the rest of the garden by roses, pink valerian (Centranthus), poppies (Papaver) and the glossy leaves of Acanthus mollis. Wisteria, Campsis and climbing roses trained up the walls and on to an overhead structure cast pools of welcome shade in summer.

The first stage in any garden planning involves taking stock of what you already have, whether it is a bare site surrounding a new house, an established garden which is in some way unsatisfactory or where the original design and planting did not take into account new conditions such as water shortages.

Along with the normal tasks of allocating areas for various uses, deciding on the direction of paths and locating features, you must also take into account all the factors contributing to dryness. Drought, whether the result of insufficient rainfall, a free-draining soil, high temperatures or a combination of all three, can be aggravated by exposure to drying winds, the rain "shadow" caused by buildings or trees, the lie of the land or simply the absence of shade. If you are new to the area and are in doubt as to why your new garden seems dry, it is worth talking to gardening neighbors and checking on the annual precipitation with the local weather station.

The most dominant feature in any garden is almost certain to be the house. From a practical point of view you have to consider access—the coming and going of people and vehicles—while aesthetically the character of the house could have a very strong influence on the styling of the garden.

Consider, too, the water-collecting potential of your house and any outbuildings. The humble rainwater butt is not to be despised but a large galvanized water storage tank will have a much greater capacity. It can be sited and screened to prevent it being an eyesore. A much more expensive option is to use a large fiberglass receptacle, such as a domestic septic tank, for the bulk storage of water underground. It will have to be connected to the roof guttering and provided with an overflow taken to a soakaway, or an automatic shut-off valve to stop it overfilling; the water is normally made available for use by means of an electric pump.

RIGHT *It is advisable to cut a steep slope into a series of terraces, if finances will allow, so that rainwater will be trapped, erosion prevented and cultivation made easier. Here, stone retaining walls provide opportunities to display plants like the purple lavender and a tub of Agapanthus.*

From the point of view of planning, the most important plants on the site are those which are too large or well established to transplant, be they trees or shrubs. These will either have to be worked into your design or removed. Forest trees like chestnuts, sycamores and poplars are very thirsty and have dense or long, questing roots. Their removal might release moisture for more desirable plants but a tree should only be condemned after much careful thought and inspection, and only if you are certain that it is not the subject of a preservation order made by the local authorities. Do not remove a tree simply because it is old. Gnarled and bent specimens are full of character and will provide an established look to a new garden. Established shrubs that have developed deep tap roots, for example *Cistus*, ceanothus and brooms, prove practically impossible to move.

The lay of the land

Next consider the steepness and direction of any slopes and assess the natural draining patterns. On a steep slope water will almost certainly drain away rapidly. If the slope can be cut into a series of terraces, more of the rainfall will soak into the soil. Any additional water applied to the highest terrace will gently filter down to each of the lower ones in turn. Gentle slopes will direct water toward beds and borders, while by creating a slight hollow we can ensure that water is absorbed into a particular area, perhaps to benefit a favorite tree. Where periods of drought are broken by sudden torrential downpours, catchment areas are to be recommended—in some lands they are actually required by law. These consist of a series of holes which are then filled with gravel. When it rains, water runs into the holes and gradually permeates the surrounding soil.

Terraces in the vicinity of the house are best retained by walls of brick, stone or timber; further away they can be linked with banks—but remember that a sunny bank will lose moisture rapidly. If it is steep, there is a risk of erosion for in a downpour water does not sink into dry soil; instead it runs off, washing away the topsoil. If this is a serious problem, the bank can be stabilized with special plastic netting, available from hardware stores, and secured with long pegs. Holes are then made in the netting for ground-cover shrubs like junipers, *Cistus*, *Hypericum*, *Centranthus* and *Genista*. An alternative is to use rock to create a series of outcrops, with spaces left for plants. Where the slope is less steep and rainfall adequate, it can be covered in grass.

Unattractive views can be screened and unwelcome noise reduced by mounding up soil, but in the dry garden you must think hard before doing this, particularly if the soil is naturally free-draining—a man-made mound is certain to be drier than the surrounding land.

Making changes to existing levels is hard work if you do it yourself, expensive if you employ a contractor, particularly when the site is inaccessible to soil-moving machinery. The work does not consist simply of taking some soil off here and putting it down there. First of all you will have to dig off and make a stack of the topsoil, that precious surface layer which contains everything we have to offer our plants and which can vary considerably in thickness. Then you have to move the subsoil about to achieve the new contours before replacing the topsoil.

As a result, most people have to settle for making only minor changes to levels, which means that the present shape of your land will influence the style and planning of your garden. A hilly site may preclude a formal design that requires a series of level planes to work properly. It would, however, be ideal for a semi-wild garden with paths winding through drifts of shrubs, hardy plants and bulbs.

If there is a crossfall along a main line of vision, you can try to reduce the impression that the land is slipping sideways by planting tall subjects on the lower side and shorter ones on the upper.

Microclimates

Every garden is influenced by the local climate but in addition the positioning of buildings, walls, trees and large shrubs, the aspect and even the slope produce slight variations, making each individual garden—even a dry one—a series of microclimates. A small city garden, for example, may be surrounded by high buildings which will shade it from direct

sunlight and rain-bearing winds, resulting in spindly plants short of moisture and drawn up in their search for light. Conversely, such a garden can become a sun-trap and, at times, uncomfortably hot.

The shade produced by a wall, pleasantly cool or unpleasantly cold depending on the general climate, creates very different growing conditions from the ground exposed to the reflected sunlight on the other side. You need to observe, therefore, the patterns of sun and shadow on your plot and how these vary according to the seasons and time of day. Soil that is bathed in sunshine throughout the middle of the day will be drier than that which receives only morning or evening sunshine. In winter, when the sun is low in the sky, shadows will stretch far longer than they do during the months of summer.

In my own garden a strip under a shady wall receives no sun at all and a considerable area adjoining it is in shade for months on end. Strange as

A shady wall painted in a light color will make a garden seem brighter while providing a good background for flowers of dark or muted coloring, such as these foxgloves (Digitalis purpurea Excelsior Hybrids) and the vigorous rambler rose 'Veilchenblau.'

The microclimate created by this high rock face has been exploited for the warmth, shelter and shade it provides. The seat, which is shaded during the hottest part of the day, is flanked by Chusan palms (Chamaerops humilis). *If the general climate of the area precludes the use of such tender plants, they could be replaced with the hardier* Trachycarpus fortunei. *The low walls are clad in* Hedera canariensis *and the terra-cotta urns planted with* Echeveria.

this may seem, from the point of view of planting this has more advantages than drawbacks. I can grow real shade-loving plants near the wall, while a little further out I have shrubs like magnolias and tree peonies whose spring blossoms are liable to damage by frost, especially if they are then touched by early-morning sun. Being in shade, mine flower a week or two later than they would in a more open position, which means they are likely to escape the frosts as well as being shielded from the morning sun. Later in the year they receive plenty of sunshine which encourages them to set flower buds.

In addition to cutting down on light, walls, trees and buildings can cast a rain shadow where the soil will be much drier than in other parts of the garden. A canopy of trees, for example, can prevent as much as three-quarters of rainfall from reaching the ground. To return again to my shady border, it would be reasonable to expect it to be damp but in

fact it is as dry as many of my sunny borders because the wall provides shelter from the main rain-bearing winds. Only on still, wet days when raindrops fall vertically does it get a real soaking.

The frost pocket is another possible hazard to consider. Like water, cold air flows downhill until it collects in a hollow or valley, or until it meets a barrier in the form of a wall, hedge or fence. These areas, known as frost pockets or hollows, are prone to early, late and more prolonged frosts. If your garden is on a hillside, make sure you leave gaps in any solid planting on the lower side of the garden to allow the cold air to escape, or carefully arrange the planting of very hardy subjects at the top of the slope to deflect the flow. Should your garden be in an actual frost hollow, all you can do is avoid planting particularly tender species. Otherwise, each autumn you will need to wrap such shrubs in straw or bracken and cover deciduous plants with an extra layer of mulch.

A sunny bank

A bank need not be just a grassy slope between one level area and another, difficult and sometimes dangerous to mow; if attractively planted, it can become a garden feature in its own right. For a steep or high bank, it is advisable to restrict the choice of plants to fast-growing ground cover and to set them closer together than normal.

Start the planting at the top of the slope and work downward, creating a hollow for each plant as this will make watering easier. For trees and large shrubs, you may need to make mini terraces, retaining the outer edge with wooden planks or railroad ties, which are held in place by pegs driven into the bank. If the soil is shallow, replace the subsoil in each plant's position with a mixture of topsoil and compost or manure. This bank is shown in early summer.

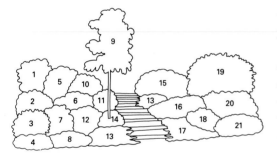

1 *Rosa rugosa* 'Alba': 5 ft. tall, sturdy wild rose, with deeply veined leaves and large, single, white flowers produced continuously and followed by large red hips.

2 *Lupinus arboreus* (tree lupin): fast-growing evergreen shrub, 4 ft. tall, with spires of scented yellow flowers over elegant, fingered leaves in summer.

3 *Cotoneaster microphyllus*: small, dark, evergreen leaves clothe the arching branches of this wide-spreading shrub which will reach a height of 2½ ft. The early summer flowers, resembling miniature hawthorn blooms, are followed by red berries.

4 *Halimiocistus wintonensis* 'Merrist Wood Cream': slightly tender, 2 ft. tall, evergreen shrub with grayish leaves and single pale yellow flowers with maroon centers which are produced in early summer.

5 *Hypericum* 'Hidcote': 5 ft. tall, semi-evergreen shrub, covered in shallow, saucer-shaped, golden flowers in late summer.

6 *Ceanothus thyrsiflorus repens*: quickly forms a wide mound of dense evergreen foliage, 3 ft. high; soft blue flowers in late spring.

7 *Genista lydia*: 2 ft. tall deciduous shrub with arching green shoots bearing innumerable small yellow flowers in late spring or early summer.

8 *Juniperus communis* 'Repanda': initially prostrate, this wide-spreading, dark green juniper gradually grows to 1 ft.

9 *Betula pendula* 'Dalecarlica' (Swedish birch): smooth white trunk and gracefully pendulous twigs hung with fern-like leaves; it makes a narrow-headed tree, unlikely to get much taller than 33 ft. on dry soils.

10 *Phlomis fruticosa* (Jerusalem sage): evergreen shrub, 2½ ft. tall, with gray leaves and whorls of hooded yellow flowers from early to midsummer.

11 *Lonicera pileata*: dense, ground-covering evergreen shrub with small dark green leaves and inconspicuous tiny cream flowers in early summer and purple berries.

12 *Prunus laurocerasus* 'Otto Luyken': narrow pointed leaves on ascending branches make this a distinctive laurel, 3 ft. tall but wide-spreading; white flowers appear in spring and red fruits, which turn black, are produced in autumn.

13 *Hedera helix* 'Green Ripple': a good ivy for ground cover in sunny positions with small, bright green, deeply indented leaves with prominent pale green veins.

14 *Armeria maritima* 'Vindictive': free-flowering thrift with spherical heads of deep pink flowers in early summer on 4 in. stems which rise from dense clumps of evergreen, grass-like leaves.

15 *Cistus × corbariensis* (syn. *C. × hybridus*): pink buds open to small, single, white flowers with a yellow center in early summer on this reasonably hardy, dense, 2½ ft. tall evergreen shrub.

16 *Lavandula vera*: this lavender has comparatively broad silver leaves and makes a broad bush, 2½ ft. tall; strongly scented, blue-gray flowers on long stalks are produced in late summer.

17 *Hedera helix* 'Manda's Crested': medium-sized, wavy edged leaves, some of which turn a coppery red in autumn.

18 *Centranthus ruber atrococcineus*: a fine form of valerian with rich red flowers on 2½ ft. stems in early summer over clumps of fleshy leaves; evergreen perennial.

19 *Cytisus* 'Zeelandia': broom with arching shoots smothered in early summer with cream and lilac-pink flowers; deciduous shrub which will reach a height of 5 ft.

20 *Rosa × jacksonii* 'Max Graf': wide-spreading, prostrate rose, making a dense carpet of glossy foliage; single, pink, scented flowers appear in summer.

21 *Nepeta* 'Six Hills Giant': large and stronger than the usual catmint, this 2½ ft. tall herbaceous perennial has dark gray leaves and lavender-blue flowers in early summer; if pruned after the first flowering, it will flower again in late summer.

TREES AND SHRUBS
FOR COASTAL
WINDBREAKS
The following plants
would make effective
windbreaks in a coastal
garden. Those marked ◆
are frost-hardy and may
be damaged in very
severe conditions.
Acer pseudoplatanus
Crataegus persimilis
  'Prunifolia'
◆ *Cupressus macrocarpa*
Elaeagnus species
◆ *Escallonia* species
Euonymus japonicus
Fraxinus excelsior
◆ *Griselinia littoralis*
Hebe brachysiphon
Hippophae rhamnoides
◆ *Olearia* × *macrodonta*
Pinus contorta latifolia
◆ *Pinus radiata*
Populus alba
Prunus spinosa
◆ *Quercus ilex*
Tamarix species
Ulex europaeus

The wind factor

All locations have a prevailing wind and the shape of the land as well as buildings and trees can funnel it and break it into currents, sending it eddying and twisting like water. Wind patterns are less easy to evaluate and less predictable than many other natural phenomena, but it is worth spending some time on windy days finding out which are the drafty spots and where shelter already exists. Observe if the existing trees lean in a particular direction.

All plants draw in water through their roots and transpire it from their leaves. A fast-moving wind causes transpiration at a faster rate and at the same time dries out the soil leaving the roots short of water. This dehydrating effect can be reduced by setting up a windbreak. A drying wind, be it cold or warm, is the most damaging, particularly for an exposed country garden. In the coastal garden, it is the gale-force winds carrying salt and even sand that do the most damage, killing young growth, scorching foliage, bending and even uprooting plants.

The best sort of windbreak, whether by the ocean or inland, is a permeable barrier which allows some wind to percolate at a reduced speed, rather than a wall or solid fence which deflects the wind over the top and around the ends causing damaging turbulence on the inside of the wall. Living screens of trees and shrubs present the best appearance and in time will make a tall shelter belt, but they can take up

A garden on a coastal inlet is unlikely to be as exposed as one facing the full fury of ocean gales and will allow pines and other trees to grow to the water's edge. The strong light and absence of hard frosts provide the ideal conditions for rosemary, Euphorbia *and pink* Lavatera, *seen here with clipped box topiary. The stone walls give the plants added protection.*

The golden Juniperus chinensis aurea *and the* birch (Betula) *in this exposed Tasmanian garden give some indication of the direction of the prevailing wind. In the foreground low-growing plants, including blue* Convolvulus sabatius, *purple-pink thrift* (Armeria), *pink* Dianthus, *yellow* Achillea *and dusky pink* Helianthemum, *flank a path which is carpeted with mat-forming* Sedum acre 'Aureum.'

shrubs. In very exposed positions, the trees (if deciduous) must be planted as "whips," which means they will be only about 3 ft. tall. If you are using conifers, it is best to purchase small, container-grown specimens. Do not buy older plants as they need to acclimatize and make good roots.

The soil

The soil will control the nature of your garden every bit as much as the climate. It may be heavy or light, acid or alkaline, shallow or deep, rich or barren. It may be solely because you are on sand or gravel that your garden is dry, but it is possible to make improvements. Because it is so important to understand your soil and know how best to improve it, the subject is discussed at length in the next chapter, "Down to earth" (see page 33). Here, my concern is how soil might affect the design of the garden.

The soil will most certainly control which plants will grow best and, thus, it may affect its styling. For instance, it is no good planning to fill formal box-edged beds with modern hybrid tea roses, fuchsias or dahlias if your garden is on hungry sand, unless you take steps to improve it; instead you will have to consider using *rugosa* roses, lavender, *Santolina* or pelargoniums. A design in which a large immaculate lawn is intended to be the main feature would not be wise unless you can depend on irrigation (see pages 28 and 49). Nor is a woodland garden a good idea. Dry shade is the most inhospitable environment and the number of species that you will be able to grow will steadily reduce as the trees develop and take most of the available moisture. If you have an acid soil, it would be far better to create a moorland scene with a scattering of birch and mountain ash, and clumps of gorse and broom rising from a carpet of heathers or, if you live in a milder climate, make your own maquis, using drifts of *Cistus*, rosemary, marjoram and lavender.

The existing vegetation of the site should indicate the nature of the soil and the extent of the drought problem. Weeds like sorrel and storksbill suggest a sandy soil; a lawn infested with yarrow and members of the clover family indicate drought. If summer-flowering heathers or *Cytisus scoparius* (common broom) are flourishing, the soil is acid.

valuable land and compete for moisture with the very plants they are required to shelter. Where space is very limited a slatted wooden fence with narrow gaps between horizontal boards is reasonably effective. Various types of plastic netting designed to cut down wind speed are also available. Fixed to posts, the netting is especially useful as temporary protection while the shelter belt is growing.

A tall hedge, ideally one that is not too solid, will protect a small garden. A larger garden will need a row of trees, preferably evergreens, planted 3 to 4 ft. apart. Some trees, especially pines, become bare at the base in time so it is advisable to plant shade-tolerant shrubs along one side of the shelter belt, allowing a gap of 6 ft. between the trees and the

Deciding on your requirements

This colonial-style garden in New York will appeal to those who like formality and neatness combined with romantic touches, such as the rose tumbling over the arch and along the picket fence. The box-edged bed is planted with alternate triangles of Santolina and colorful bedding plants.

The second stage in planning is to decide what you would like the garden to contain—a pool, perhaps, or a pergola, a mixed shrub and herbaceous border and maybe a vegetable plot. Do you need a lawn and, if so, how big should it be (see also page 28)? Will you want an outdoor seating area, space for games, a shed, a clothesline, a compost heap? Except for the tiniest plot, the owner of every garden where drought could be a problem should convert kitchen waste, weeds, plant remains and fallen leaves into valuable compost to improve the soil's texture (see page 36). How about including an area where woody prunings can be heaped pending their reduction, via a shredder, to a moisture-trapping mulch?

Whether your garden is used primarily as a place for relaxation or to cultivate all your favorite plants, the climate is of utmost importance as it affects your basic garden planning as well as controlling which plants you grow successfully. If you choose to have an outdoor seating area, its location will be dictated by the amount of sunshine, its intensity throughout the seasons and where it falls. If the number of warm days is limited, choose somewhere facing the sun at midday. A paved dining area set against a wall will absorb the heat and release it as the day cools, taking the chill off the evening air. For those few uncomfortably hot days, it is sufficient to have a seat or two in the dappled shade of a tree or pergola.

It may be that you are never happier than when busy about the garden, but do you find that other commitments or the onward march of time limit what you can do? Is it the result of your labor rather than the labor itself which you love, be it a perfect bloom heavy with scent, a fig plucked warm from the wall or a picture made with living plants? There are, I suspect, far more who love gardens than love gardening. This is not a sin but, unless you can afford a gardener, it means that planning and organization for easy maintenance must have priority. Once the garden is established, the work should be no more irksome than the routine dusting and vacuuming that goes on day by day inside the house. This will have a bearing on whether or not you decide to install irrigation (see page 46). An automated system of watering will save many hours, especially if you are starting a garden from scratch.

Choosing a style

A dry garden can be in any style. The house, the site or the surroundings might indicate which is the best to choose, but in the end the choice must be yours. If you are the proud owner of an old cottage, then it would seem almost obligatory to have a traditional cottage garden with hollyhocks, honeysuckle and lots of herbs. A more formal house might suggest a corresponding formal garden with straight lines, level surfaces linked by steps and a good deal of symmetry—twinned bay trees, pairs of cypresses and a rectangular or circular pool. A modern house, all glass and concrete panels, would look entirely wrong in a garden which was strongly influenced by designs from the past. It would either require a contemporary approach with clean architectural lines and plants of strong form and texture like yuccas and junipers, and perhaps a water mobile in stainless steel, or it could appear to inhabit a near natural landscape with

The author's garden, which needed to be in sympathy with an old house, combines a firm structure with luxuriant planting. In late spring, it is lit by the yellow heads of Euphorbia characias wulfenii 'Lambrook Gold' which face the contrasting Berberis thunbergii 'Rose Glow.' Mauve Wisteria sinensis clambers up the walls of the house, bringing additional color.

groups of native trees and face a meadow rich with drought-tolerant wild flowers. Most of us, however, live in houses of no great architectural merit or sense of period, which is an advantage in that it allows us to choose a style that suits us personally.

If you like order, strong and easily perceived patterns, you will want a formal style with a plan based on straight lines and circles and a good deal of symmetry and plants arranged in rows and blocks. Should you prefer a more relaxed, "cottagey" effect, begin with a similar strong simple framework but soften the hard lines with a profusion of plants including lots of self-seeders like honesty *(Lunaria)*, foxglove *(Digitalis)* and opium poppy *(Papaver somniferum)*. Allow the prolific and long-flowering pink-and-white *Erigeron karvinskianus*—christened by a friend "daisy gone crazy"—to colonize the cracks between paving slabs.

Because your garden shares the feature of dryness with gardens of Islamic and Mediterranean countries, you could have some fun by creating in a separate enclosure a Moorish patio with a pool and splashing fountain or an Italian-style terrace, all stone or terra-cotta-colored paving, a shady pergola, bright pelargoniums, clipped box, a narrow cypress or two and big earthenware pots filled (if you have a frost-free greenhouse or conservatory for their winter home) with citrus trees, daturas and oleanders.

You may prefer complete informality, wanting your garden to echo nature, aided and controlled, of course, but still recognizable as nature. For you, there is the wild garden consisting either of a mixture of exotic and native plants, or devoted solely to wild flowers. A mini-cornfield is one option, planted with cereals, annual grasses mixed with poppies *(Papaver)*, corncockle *(Agrostemma githago)*, pheasant's eye *(Adonis annua)* and cornflower *(Centaurea cyanus)*. On a poor, sandy soil with little water you could have a wild flower lawn, the sparse grasses providing a perfect setting for yarrow *(Achillea millefolium)*, wild carrot *(Daucus carota)*, sheep's bit *(Jasione laevis)*, chamomile *(Chamaemelum nobile)* and harebell *(Campanula rotundifolia)*.

An outdoor room

The plants for this terrace or patio border, seen here in early autumn, have been chosen to create a warm Mediterranean atmosphere, with aromatic foliage and flowers filling the air with fragrance. Several of the shrubs are somewhat tender and will need walls to reflect the heat of the sun and protect them from cold drying winds. In very cold areas or really severe weather, it is advisable to move the containers inside and protect the more susceptible shrubs marked ◆ by surrounding them with plastic windbreak netting or a frost blanket.

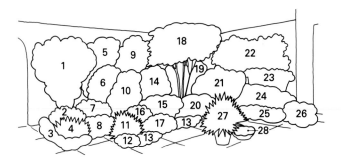

1 ◆ *Aloysia triphylla* (lemon verbena): grown not for its small, pale mauve flowers in late summer and autumn but for its pale green leaves which emit a wonderful scent of lemons when crushed; trained on a warm wall, it can reach a height of 8 ft.

2 ◆ *Rosmarinus officinalis* 'Benenden Blue' (rosemary): spring-flowering, bushy evergreen, 5 ft. tall, with highly aromatic, slender leaves; in this very beautiful form the leaves are a darker green and the flowers a rich blue.

3 *Stachys byzantina* 'Silver Carpet': this non-flowering form of lamb's ears with woolly gray leaves makes good ground cover.

4 *Sisyrinchium striatum* 'Aunt May': evergreen perennial with tufts of iris-like leaves striped in pale yellow and green; narrow spires of creamy flowers, 1½ ft. tall, appear in early summer, followed by black seed pods.

5 *Robinia hispida* (box acacia): deciduous shrub, best trained against a wall where it will reach 10 ft.; the late-spring flowers resemble pink wisteria among the young, bronzy, pinnate foliage.

6 ◆ *Myrtus communis* (common myrtle): aromatic, densely leaved evergreen which will grow to 10 ft. tall against a warm wall; small white flowers appear in late summer, followed by black berries.

7 ◆ *Coronilla valentina* 'Citrina': dense, rounded shrub, 6 ft. tall, with glaucous leaves and scented primrose-yellow flowers in late spring, with a lesser flowering following in the autumn.

8 *Epilobium canum*: sprawling, 1 ft. tall, herbaceous perennial; gray leaves and scarlet, trumpet-shaped flowers are produced from late summer into autumn.

9 *Vitis vinifera* 'Purpurea' (claret vine): compact hardy grape with soft purple leaves which turn dark red in autumn when small dark blue, bitter grapes are freely produced.

10 ◆ *Olearia stellulata* 'De Candolle': compact daisy bush, 6 ft. tall, with small gray leaves and white flowers in late spring.

11 *Yucca filamentosa* 'Bright Edge': rosettes of 2 ft. tall, green and yellow striped, sword-like leaves from which taller spires of waxy, white bell flowers rise in late summer.

12 *Thymus* 'Doone Valley': lemon-scented thyme forming dense 2 in. high mats with dark green leaves splashed with gold, often tinged red in winter; purple flowers are produced in late summer.

13 *Helianthemum* 'Rhodanthe Carneum': sprawling, 1 ft. tall, evergreen shrub with gray leaves and smothered with orange-centered, pink flowers in early summer, followed by a few later blooms.

14 *Abelia × grandiflora*: semi-evergreen shrub
5 ft. tall with small burnished leaves and
flesh-pink, funnel-shaped flowers in late
summer and autumn.

15 *Nerine bowdenii*: autumn-flowering bulb
producing long-lasting clusters of pink starry
flowers on 1½ ft. stems; the strap-like leaves
do not arrive until after the flowers.

16 ◆ *Punica granatum nana*: dwarf
pomegranate, 3 ft. tall; vermilion flowers and
orange fruits in early autumn; the young
leaves are coppery when emerging and change
to yellow before they fall.

17 *Ceratostigma willmottianum*: 2½ ft. tall
deciduous shrub; clusters of small, bright
blue flowers in late summer and autumn,
followed by reddish-brown seed heads.

18 *Aralia elata*: sparsely branched deciduous
tree, 13 ft. tall, with spiny stems and large
leaves clustered at their apex; plumes of cream

flowers crown the tree in autumn.

19 ◆ *Pittosporum* 'Garnettii': upright, 10 ft.
tall, evergreen, with gray-green leaves
margined with white, flushed pink in winter.

20 *Santolina pinnata*: fragrant, silvery white,
feathery leaves cover this 2½ ft. tall, mound-
shaped sub-shrub; lemon-yellow, button-like
flowers appear in summer.

21 *Euphorbia characias wulfenii* 'Lambrook
Gold': evergreen shrubby spurge with 3 ft.
long, bottle brush-like stems clothed in gray-
green leaves; big heads of green-yellow
flowers develop slowly in spring.

22 ◆ *Ceanothus* 'Burkwoodii': glossy-leaved
evergreen growing to 10 ft. on a wall; when
pruned in spring, deep blue, delicately
scented flowers appear in summer and autumn.

23 *Amaryllis belladonna*: pink and white
trumpet-shaped flowers, smelling of apricots,
bloom on 2 ft. tall purple stems in early

autumn, after the leaves have died away.

24 *Ruta graveolens* 'Jackman's Blue': neat
evergreen bush, 2 ft. tall, grown for its blue-
gray filigree foliage (see also page 116).

25 *Origanum laevigatum* 'Herrenhausen':
unscented marjoram with dark green leaves
and clusters of tiny purple flowers on 1 ft.
wiry stems in late summer and autumn.

26 *Convolvulus cneorum*: silvery leaves with a
silky sheen and white, funnel-shaped flowers,
shaded on the outside with pink, add up to a
delightful, 2 ft. tall, evergreen shrub; flowers
in late spring and sometimes autumn.

27 *Cordyline australis* 'Torbay Dazzler': half-
hardy evergreen with long, narrow, sharply
pointed, green-and-white-striped leaves.

28 *Echeveria secunda*: tender perennial
succulent; light jade-green leaves; red-and-
yellow flowers on 4 in. stems are produced in
late summer.

Developing the plan

A richly textured carpet of Cotoneaster dammeri *mixed with the small-leaved ivy* Hedera helix 'Glacier' *makes a low-maintenance alternative to grass. It will not turn brown during a drought, nor will it become thin and patchy as the multi-stemmed birch* Betula albosinensis *develops.*

With the preliminary work completed, now is the time to take tracing paper and, over a scale plan of the site, experiment with designs for your garden. The plan should show the boundaries, the house with its doors and main windows and the positions of trees, as well as indicating any good views or eyesores that need screening, the direction of the main winds, sunny and shady areas, the overhang of trees and steep slopes. This will enable you to decide on the best positions for the main outdoor living area, where you need a windbreak and where shading is desirable. It will also indicate the best areas for planting. Next, with your list of requirements, identify positions for your pond, pergola, shed and so on and consider how they will interlink.

Deciding about a lawn

Give as much thought to the lawn as any other feature. Too often it is made up of whatever land is left over after everything else has been made so that it has no definite shape of its own. In areas where grass has to be irrigated and water is in short supply, a lawn should never be larger than strictly necessary for family needs and it should be placed where most useful. Remember that highly manicured grass, if it is to remain green, demands more water than any other planting. By contrast, grass that is allowed to grow taller, as in a pasture, needs less water than other parts of the garden. Even where rainfall is more plentiful, a good lawn needs constant maintenance (see page 45) and a small lawn of strong, simple shape positioned within a framework of planting and paving will have just as much impact as a large expanse of grass. A very small patch of grass, however, of the sort often seen in city gardens, badly worn because of over-use and too much shading, should be avoided altogether and replaced with paving or gravel. You should also consider the style of your garden. If, for example, you decide to exploit the dryness of your soil and create a Mediterranean garden, it would be a mistake to include a lawn.

Alternatives to closely mown grass for carpeting the garden consist of ground-cover plants, hard materials such as brick and concrete, softer ones like gravel, crushed stone, timber and bark chippings, and rough grass which requires only occasional cutting and minimal or no irrigation. Where mown grass is provided solely for its smooth, even appearance, a low, dense, ground-covering plant can be substituted. A few of these like dwarf thymes and snow-in-summer (*Cerastium tomentosum*) will take a limited amount of foot traffic. In other parts of the garden where a uniform texture is not necessary, a mixture of low shrubs and mixed ground cover—ivy, *Euonymus*, *Helianthemum*—will provide more interest and color than an uninterrupted expanse of grass, and need not require more maintenance if any bare soil is covered with a mulch to suppress weeds and conserve moisture (see page 41).

Eryngium giganteum
Introduced from the Middle East in the nineteenth century, this biennial sea holly gained its popular name of "Miss Willmott's Ghost" from the famous Edwardian gardener Ellen Willmott, who would secretly scatter its seed when visiting the gardens of friends. In the spring after sowing, celandine-like plants with deep tap roots appear. A year or two later, spectral, gray flowerheads crown the 2–3 ft. tall plants, creating a most dramatic feature in the dry garden and providing excellent material for both fresh and dried flower arrangements. The thistle flowers appear in mid- to late summer after which time the plant dies, usually leaving behind so many self-sown seedlings that they may need to be thinned.

Paving and gravel

In the past, materials like paving or gravel were used solely for practical purposes in providing a dry, clean surface and, to a lesser extent, for linking buildings to the living parts of the garden. Only recently have they been treated as a garden feature in their own right. In the dry garden they have additional virtues: they keep the soil cool, reduce evaporation and can direct water to where it is most needed.

When it comes to choosing paving, take into account the character and age of your house in order to achieve unity. Natural sandstone is the first choice where there is a fine period house, but it is very expensive and difficult to lay. Fortunately, there are now much cheaper and easier-to-handle man-made slabs which imitate stone quite successfully. Brick paving looks handsome in almost every situation and its small size makes it suitable for curves and circles. Granite cobblestones create a rougher texture and are particularly suitable for urban gardens. Precast concrete slabs come in all sizes, surface textures and colors. Keep to those colors which approximate to natural stone and bear in mind that pale colors, though fine in soft light, can produce a glare in bright sunshine. Poured concrete is useful in that it can be cast into any shape you want. A coloring agent can be added at the mixing stage, while an overall pattern can be produced by introducing bands of brickwork which have the added advantage of providing the expansion joints that are necessary every 10–13 ft. A rough, non-slip surface can be given to concrete if the aggregate within it is exposed by watering and brushing the surface just before it sets. Patterns can also be stamped into the surface by the use of special tools. Remember that non-porous paving should be tilted slightly when it is laid so that rainwater percolates into the adjoining plant beds, providing them with additional moisture.

Gravel has been employed for garden paths and courtyards for centuries. It looks good, covers awkward shapes, comes in several colors and textures and is relatively cheap. It is also self-draining, and keeps the soil beneath it cool and moist. The usual complaints advanced against gravel are that it gets transferred to house or lawn on damp shoes and that it can be difficult to walk on. The first results if stones of a very small size are used and the latter when too thick a layer has been laid.

Because gravel, shingle and bark (see below) can be used as a mulch between plants as well as a surfacing for foot traffic, where a feeling of integration is desirable there is no need for a firm demarcation between plant beds and open spaces. In fact, most plants, bulbs and shrubs can be planted through a 4 in. layer of gravel.

Much larger, sea-washed pebbles and rocks are just as effective in reducing evaporation and preventing weeds and they can make a real contribution to the landscape. A few large, rounded boulders grouped with suitable plants can be just as eye-catching as a piece of garden sculpture.

Where a still more informal effect is required, as in woodland, coarse bark chippings are a useful alternative to gravel. They make a quiet, soft surface which is pleasant to walk on and, as long as the soil beneath is well drained, will last for two or three years before needing to be topped off.

Decking

In hot climates stone and concrete surfaces especially can heat up if exposed to the sun, making them uncomfortable for people while increasing the evaporation rate, which is bad for plants. This does not happen to the same extent with timber, which is doubtless one of the reasons why decking has become so popular for terraces and patios in the U.S. and Australia. Other advantages are that it does not reflect heat and light into the house, allows water to reach the soil beneath it, is warmer on the days when concrete is cold, is softer under foot and blends with much modern architecture and with plants. In the damp climate of many parts of Europe, timber is liable to become slippery but for a garden which is dry because of low rainfall, decking is worth considering as long as it is sited where it receives the maximum amount of sunshine.

Choosing the plants

Having arrived at a satisfactory overall plan, the next stage is to choose the plants that will bring the whole scheme to life. Your first objective is to select plants that fulfill the needs of the design; the second objective, which is of equal importance, is to give each plant, as far as you possibly can, the conditions it likes best, be that sun or shade, maximum shelter or complete exposure to the elements. In the dry garden this also means allocating any areas that are comparatively moist, or easiest to water, to those plants least able to withstand drought.

There should also be harmony in the planting. This is best achieved by not having too many different kinds of plant and by grouping them according to their cultural needs—plants that have adapted to shady woodland conditions simply do not look right sitting next to sun lovers.

Before starting to draw up a planting scheme, it is helpful to compile lists of the plants most suited to the soil and climate, not alphabetically but according to the function for which they are best fitted, and then make a selection from them. Their size, year-round good appearance, longevity and hardiness may qualify some plants to form part of the permanent living structure of the garden. A few will have such a dramatic outline, leaf, stem or branch shape that they can be used to create a focal point; others will be suitable for clothing walls and fences or decorating pergolas and trellises. Color, if provided by foliage or bark, is not fleeting like that of flowers so the plants that will provide it need to be considered before the shrubs and hardy perennials grown primarily for their flowers. Annuals are grown almost solely for the bright splashes of color which they bring. This and their transient nature puts them into a category of their own. Bulbs, hopefully, will be long-lived but because they put in an appearance for such a short time they are best used as a finishing touch, when all the other decorative planting is in place. More information on choosing the plants and how to use them is provided in the later chapter "Plants for the dry garden" (see page 53).

In hot, dry, frost-free countries, cacti, orange-flowered aloes, agaves and Opuntia *can make a dramatic landscape without the need for irrigation. Lawns, on the other hand, will need frequent watering to keep them lush and green.*

Grouped around the potted Pelargonium *'Frank Headley' is an assortment of plants. Some of these are fully hardy in temperate regions, including the pink* Geranium sanguineum, *fleshy-leaved* Bergenia, *spotted-leaved* Pulmonaria *and the shrubby* Spiraea *'Goldflame.' Others like the purple* Lavandula stoechas *will take only a few degrees of frost.*

Zoning

An important design element of xeriscaping (see page 11) is known as "zoning." This has two main principles: reducing or eliminating thirsty areas of grass and replacing them with hard surfacing, gravel or ground-cover plants such as ivy *(Hedera)*, *Geranium*, *Euonymus* and sun roses *(Helianthemum)*, and the grouping together of plants whose water requirements are as nearly identical as possible so that irrigation can be more effective.

In the arid parts of the United States many gardens are divided into zones, each of which receives a different amount of irrigation. The area provided with most water is called the "oasis" zone and normally adjoins the house, in order to provide it with a cool green setting. It contains the lawn and those plants that need continual moisture. The "intermediate" zone is used for plants that only require help in the hottest, driest months, and the third—furthest from the house—is reserved for plants that only have to be watered to get them established.

In temperate regions, we often exploit the warmer microclimate around the house in order to grow half-hardy subjects. Many of these come from hotter and also drier lands and it would be a mistake to give them extra water. The "oasis" zone, or indeed the only irrigated area, in these circumstances might be restricted to the lawn, the shrub and flower borders which adjoin it and the vegetable plot.

Zoning not only conserves water but makes for ease of maintenance. It might sound an entirely novel idea but is only an application of the good plantsperson's usual way of working with, and not against, nature.

A zoned garden In the south-facing garden illustrated here (see above), the oasis zone contains the lawn, vegetable plot and the thirstiest plants, which must have a moist soil throughout their growing season. They can be shrubs like daphnes, rhododendrons, Japanese maples and hydrangeas; herbaceous plants such as astilbes, astrantias, delphiniums, chrysanthemums, phlox and primulas; while tem-

porary bedding could include ageratums, pansies and *Impatiens*. On light soils or where the rainfall is often inadequate, this zone should be kept small.

Plants that can normally thrive on the natural rainfall but need to be given extra water during very dry and hot periods are planted in the intermediate zone. In most temperate regions these will include *Deutzia*, *Kolkwitzia*, *Weigela*, the majority of roses, *Philadelphus*, *Hebe*, *Viburnum*, lilacs and heathers, as well as *Bergenia*, *Dahlia*, Michaelmas daisies, *Rudbeckia*, *Tradescantia* and *Dianthus*.

The low water requirement zone is for plants that are naturally adapted to surviving drought and will only need watering until they are established. Most of the plants described in this book would grow well under such conditions. The microclimate of the site may allow some of the areas to contain plants originating from hotter countries, like *Teucrium*, *Rhaphiolepis* and myrtle; others will demand completely hardy subjects.

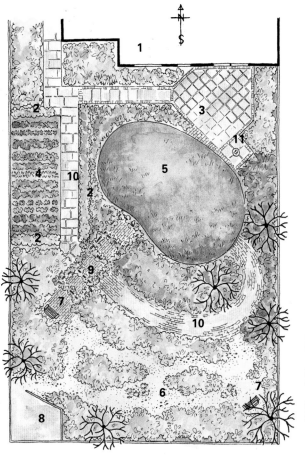

CREATING A ZONED GARDEN

When making a selection of plants for the different zones, it is essential to take into account the various characteristics of your garden which would affect the planting, such as temperature, microclimates, the nature of the soil, aspect and density of shade, if any (see pages 16–23).

- Oasis zone
- Intermediate zone
- Low water requirement zone

1 House
2 Hedge
3 Patio
4 Vegetable plot
5 Lawn
6 Gravel
7 Seat
8 Compost heap
9 Pergola
10 Path
11 Ornament

DOWN TO EARTH

A soil that too rapidly loses whatever moisture it receives, whether in the form of rain from heaven or irrigation from a sprinkler, is, after climate, the second major factor in the dry garden. Fortunately, a dry soil can be improved: its capacity to hold moisture can be increased and surface evaporation reduced. In addition, you can take measures to ensure that any watering you do is effective and efficient.

If shrub roses are to flourish in a naturally dry soil, plenty of organic matter needs to be incorporated, both before planting and in the form of a mulch. White foxgloves and blue Campanula persicifolia *are not as demanding, although they will grow taller and remain longer in flower if the soil has been enriched. While the roses and foxgloves dislike an alkaline soil, the hybrid pinks (Dianthus) in the foreground are real lime-lovers, although they will grow in all but very acid soils.*

Understanding the soil

A plant's roots must have an adequate supply of air, moisture and nutrients to make healthy growth. The characteristics of soil which control the supply of these to the roots are its texture, structure and chemical composition. Soils consist of a mixture of clay, silt and sand, and their texture depends on the proportions of these, all of which are minute particles of rock, eroded and weathered over millennia. A knowledge of your soil will enable you to determine how and when to work it, what plants will have the best chance of growing successfully in it and the amount of water you need to apply and with what frequency. Either carry out a few simple tests on it yourself or have it professionally analyzed. You will certainly be able to assess what type of soil you have and measure its acidity or alkalinity yourself. A full report from a soil laboratory (for the address of one contact your local Extension Service) will tell you, in addition, about the levels of nutrients, organic matter and trace elements present, enabling you to determine what sort of fertilizers and manures to use.

With a little practice, you can estimate the relative amounts of sand, silt and clay in your soil. Take a handful or two of damp soil and rub it between finger and thumb. A sandy soil will feel gritty and, if you squeeze it into a ball in the palm of your hand, it will fall apart when you open your fist or give it a gentle prod. If the soil feels smooth but not sticky and if you can roll it into the shape of a frankfurter sausage which falls apart if you try to bend it, you have a silty loam. A clay soil will feel very sticky and when rolled into a sausage it will bend without crumbling.

All soils have the ability to retain some moisture because it adheres to the surface of the particles. When rain falls, every soil absorbs as much water as it can, depending on its type, while the surplus continues to drain downward through the different layers of soil until it meets an impermeable layer such as rock, where it collects (see "The structure of soil," below). The uppermost level of this water is known as the water table and it can be anywhere between a few inches and hundreds of feet or more from the surface of the ground. If it is too close to the surface the result is a bog, but if it is only a few feet below and does not drop too much in summer, the roots of some plants will be able to obtain moisture from the soil which lies just above the water table in their locality. In past centuries when most people depended on wells for their water supply, everyone knew the depth of the water table. Today most of us are unaware of its very existence, but how well local

FAR RIGHT *The presence of winter- or spring-flowering heathers like this* Erica erigena *'Superba' does not necessarily indicate an acid soil for, unlike summer-flowering species, many will tolerate lime. Fine specimens of broom such as these creamy yellow* Cytisus × praecox *would, however, lead one to suspect that the soil was either neutral or acid and well drained.*

The structure of soil

Soil is made up of several distinct layers. Below the shallow, topmost layer of decaying organic matter lies the topsoil, the most fertile section of earth which sustains plant life. Usually 1–1½ ft. deep, topsoil should be well aerated and drained. The subsoil is low in nutrients and of little value to plants. The water table is the upper surface of the underground lake that forms where rain meets an impermeable layer such as rock. Between the subsoil and bedrock there may be a layer of fragmented rock.

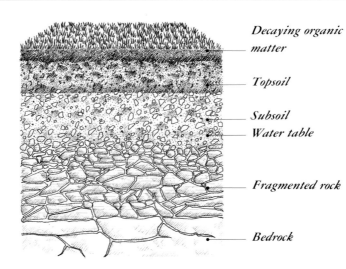

Decaying organic matter

Topsoil

Subsoil

Water table

Fragmented rock

Bedrock

SOIL PARTICLES
The particles that make up a clay soil are small, flattened and packed closely together, retaining water and excluding air. In a sandy soil the particles are larger and rounded, admitting plenty of air and allowing water to pass through rapidly. Intermediate in size are the silt particles.

Calendula officinalis
This old cottage and herb garden annual, with its pale green, aromatic leaves and orange, daisy-shaped flowers which close up at night, is able to grow in the poorest and driest soils. Known as pot marigold because at one time it was grown under glass for cutting in winter, its uses have included relieving insect stings and burns and soothing tired eyes. It has also been employed in beauty preparations—originally as a hair dye—and its petals can be included in salads and as a substitute for saffron. In recent years the color range and flower forms have been extended, and seed strains that produce fully double flowers in colors including cream and apricot are now available.

draining away, the nutrients go with it, leaving the soil impoverished. Water also carries out calcium, the presence of which makes soil alkaline or limy. As a result, sandy soil becomes progressively more acid.

Where a soil contains a high proportion of clay, the minute particles of which hold on to large amounts of water (see "The structure of soil," below), only a prolonged drought will be a problem. As the downwards movement of nutrients in clay soils is much slower than in sandy soils, clay soils are potentially much more fertile. However, from the gardener's point of view, these advantages are at considerable cost. A clay soil is very heavy to dig and can be wet and sticky in winter, and trying to cultivate it when in this condition can do more harm than good. Even walking over the surface at this time should be avoided. Slow to warm up in spring because it is short of air, by summer when it does eventually dry out it shrinks, creating cracks, and fails to absorb the rain from summer showers.

The acidity or alkalinity of soil is expressed in pH numbers on a scale of 1 (very acid) to 14 (very alkaline) with pH7 as the neutral mid-point. Moderate readings of a point both above and below pH7 will suit a wide range of plants, particularly those that do best in dry soils. Plants that like acid soils are known as calcifuges and they include rhododendrons, azaleas, camellias, fothergillas, styrax, eucryphia and most magnolias, hydrangeas and heathers. With the exception of the last, none of these is really happy on a dry soil. Simple kits for determining the pH of soils are sold in garden centers. Take samples, according to the directions given, in several parts of your garden, particularly if it is a new property as building operations may have contaminated it.

If your soil is acid, that is below 6.5, you may wish to raise it, particularly in the vegetable garden, and this is easily done by the addition of lime. Reducing alkalinity is much more difficult, however, but for a few special plants and where the soil is only slightly alkaline, it is worth applying sequestered iron or flowers of sulfur, combined with a generous dressing of organic matter.

trees cope in periods of extended drought may give some indication of its depth.

The ideal garden soil is one that has just the right mixture of clay, silt and sand. It is known to gardeners as a medium loam and is both well drained yet moist. The fertility of such a soil needs only the application of small amounts of fertilizer or organic matter to keep it in prime condition. Fortunate indeed is the owner of this paragon of soils.

A sandy soil is free-draining (see "The structure of soil," left) and likely to dry out quickly unless rain falls frequently or it is irrigated. Drought will be less of a problem, though, where there is a high water table. Sandy soils are often infertile. This is because most plant foods are only taken up by roots if they are dissolved in water, so if that water is constantly

Improving the soil

There are many beautiful plants that grow and even thrive in poor, dry, acid or alkaline sandy soil, some of which are described in the chapter "Key plants" (see pages 107–23). But even they will appreciate just a little extra moisture and feeding until their root systems have developed and they are able to look after themselves. If, however, you are not content to fill your garden solely with plants which are perfectly adapted to the type and condition of the existing soil, then you will need to improve it by adding lots of decomposing organic matter. This will be broken down into humus by the hordes of worms, bacteria, fungi and microbes which inhabit soil. The humus will lodge in the spaces between the particles of sand and slow down the movement of water and nutrients, acting rather like a sponge.

As well as improving the structure of the soil, the organic matter may also provide plants with additional nutrients including trace elements—minerals that plants need in minute quantities. The addition of organic matter simply speeds up the natural process by which dead plants and animals decompose and are absorbed back into the soil. Strange as it may seem, the best way to improve a clay soil so that it becomes warmer, better drained and easier to work is basically the same as for a sandy one.

The type of organic matter you use will depend on what is available and how much you can afford.

Compost

Homemade compost is free and gives the gardener a virtuous sense of giving back to the soil what has been taken from it, so that nothing is wasted. A pile of dead organic material, however haphazardly heaped, will eventually rot down and produce useful compost, but it may take a long time. It is better to mix less fibrous matter—weeds, cut-down plants, soft hedge trimmings, old bedding plants, grass mowings, fallen leaves and organic kitchen waste— between layers of coarser fibrous materials like thin prunings and roots. The latter material should either be chopped up first or put through a garden shredder to accelerate the rate of decomposition. From time to time, as you build up the layers, sprinkle on an activator; this can be one of those specially manufactured or anything rich in nitrogen, such as sulfate of ammonia and dried blood. The mixture needs to be damp, so water if necessary, but it is important not to overwater and get it sopping wet.

You can simply layer all the material for the compost in a heap on the ground, but it will break down faster and look neater if you make or buy a container; in any case, cover the top with polyethylene to keep out rain and keep in heat. The idea is that the decomposing matter generates enough heat over a few weeks to kill weed seeds, crop diseases and pests. Ideally, about ten days after it starts to cool, you should turn the compost, swapping the inside material with the outside material to aerate it and so start the heating cycle again, although the rise in temperature will decrease after each turning. Once the heap has cooled, it is invaded by an army of earthworms, insects and other minute animals who mix, aerate and further break down the heap.

This final phase of decomposition can take several months, and at the end your original material should be reduced to between 10–15 percent of its original volume and consist of a dark, odorless, crumbly, weed- and disease-free compost, which can either be dug into the soil or spread on the surface as a mulch.

That is the ideal, and many gardeners seem to have no problems in achieving it but others have to make do with a heap that refuses to break down completely. This hardly matters at all if your soil is sandy. Partially decayed compost is preferable to none at all but whenever possible it should be forked into the first spade's depth of soil rather than spread on the surface, mainly because of the weed seeds that will not have been killed and which will germinate. This advice is fine for a vegetable plot, or beds which are periodically cleared completely such as those devoted to annuals. But if your garden is like mine, full of trees and shrubs underplanted with ground cover or reasonably permanent herbaceous plants, then the only way of maintaining the fertility and

KITCHEN WASTE

Keep a special bin in the kitchen, with a lid, for collecting valuable kitchen waste, such as vegetable peelings, tea bags, coffee grounds, fruit and vegetable waste, even paper—although this is best shredded first—and fluff from the tumble drier. Do not use cooked food as this will attract rodents and hungry cats.

Woodland dwellers like this Arum italicum marmoratum *with creamy veins to its arrow-shaped leaves and scarlet-seeded* Iris foetidissima *appreciate a thick mulch of pulverized bark to trap moisture.*

This section through a well-made compost heap shows alternating layers of soft materials such as grass cuttings, weeds and organic kitchen waste, which are high in nitrogen, and fibrous, woody material like thin hedge prunings, leaves, straw and plant stems.

moisture-holding ability of the soil is to apply compost to the surface and leave the worms to take it down to the roots of the plants where it is needed.

I have two compost "bins"; each takes a year to fill and I leave the contents for another year before using it. I try to keep out of it pernicious weeds like the lesser celandine, quack grass, bindweed and several sorts of oxalis which were introduced to the garden by previous owners, but inevitably many get by, as do many weed seeds which are not destroyed and promptly germinate as soon as the compost is spread. There is no answer to this problem that I know of except to spread the compost over a limited area and concentrate on it, hand-weeding and treating with contact herbicide when necessary (see page 44).

Ready-made soil improvers

If you are starting a new garden, it is unlikely that you will have made any usable compost and yet this is the best opportunity you will have to incorporate manure deeply and uniformly. Even if you are only replanting a large border, you may not have enough to do any real good, for a 2 in. layer of organic matter needs to be applied and dug in. You should, therefore, look for other sources of supply.

Prepared organic manures can be purchased in bags from garden centers or by mail order. They are based on a range of materials including animal manure, vegetable waste and bark, and often have inorganic nutrients added. Although clean and convenient to use, brand-name products are expensive for large areas and may not be sufficiently bulky to make much impression on soil structure.

In the past, peat was often employed as a soil-improving material but its continued use for this purpose cannot be condoned. Raised bogs, from which most peat intended for horticulture is cut, provide a refuge for a range of rare plants, insects and birds. Few gardeners will wish to see such unique and precious habitats destroyed to make available a material which is to be used for soil improvement or as a surface mulch, especially as other organic substances work more successfully.

Manure

The traditional material for improving soil, doubtless used since agriculture began and still the best, is farmyard or stable manure. Most livestock farmers put manure back on their own land but are sometimes prepared to part with a load; more often it is worth approaching riding schools or horse owners. Manure should not appear to be made up solely of straw or other bedding, although these are desirable additives. Try to obtain well-rotted manure as fresh manure can be too strong; if you have to accept it while it is still fresh, have it tipped into a heap and wait until it has decomposed.

If you keep chickens, rabbits or pigeons, add their droppings to your compost heap, preferably mixing them with straw. Goat owners will know that one of the advantages of keeping goats, aside from the milk they give, is the value of their litter which is even richer in nutrients than horse manure.

Another source of excellent organic matter is a mushroom farm. Mushrooms are grown in a mixture of straw, horse or poultry manure and peat, to which gypsum is added. Spent mushroom compost is particularly useful on clay soils as the gypsum acts like lime and improves its structure.

Green manure

Another way to condition your soil is to incorporate green manure. This is a green crop specifically grown to be dug into the soil to provide organic matter and plant food; special green manure mixtures are available from seed merchants. If the crop occupies the ground during the winter, it will have the added advantage of protecting the soil from heavy rain which can damage its structure as well as wash away nutrients. Traditionally practiced in the vegetable plot, green manure can be used elsewhere. In a new garden, for instance, it is an ideal way to build up fertility and smother weeds before the permanent planting takes place. Dig in the crop while it is still green, but allow it to wilt first. You can either use a cultivator to churn the plants into the soil or you can chop them up with a lawn mower before digging them into a depth of about 6 in.

Especially good for improving the texture of dry, sandy soils are those plants with a dense root system which break the soil down only slowly, such as grazing rye. Also useful are those which "fix" extra nitrogen from the atmosphere—lupins, winter beans, red clover and alfalfa come into this category.

Fertilizers

While organic matter improves the soil, it does not necessarily feed your plants. If your soil is lacking an essential nutrient, it will take years before regular applications of bulky organic material will correct the loss, and you will need to add a fertilizer. Bear in mind, however, that fertilizers are supplements for organic matter, not substitutes.

The three essential plant foods are nitrogen, expressed as N, phosphorus (P) and potassium (K). Sandy soils are often low in nitrogen and potassium; if this is the case, the growth of some plants which

ABOVE *Well-manured and fertilized soil allows plants to withstand drought. Although this lawn shows signs of stress, the hostas,* Macleaya *and golden variegated* Cornus alba *'Spaethii' appear unaffected, while the* Sisyrinchium, Salvia sclarea, *silvery* Artemisia, Ruta graveolens *'Jackman's Blue' and purple* Cotinus *are doubtless enjoying the heat.*

ABOVE RIGHT *Good drainage is essential for natives of hot, dry lands, such as these colorful lavenders* (Lavandula angustifolia).

WATER-ABSORBENT POLYMERS

Until quite recently only naturally occurring materials could be used to improve the water-holding capabilities of soil but, impelled by the need to make deserts flower, scientists have succeeded in producing polyacrylamide granules which will absorb 150 times their own weight in water and release it slowly to the roots of plants. They are now available on the market but their use in gardens has tended to be limited to hanging baskets and other containers. Reports on their effectiveness are conflicting so perhaps because of their relatively high cost you may be wise to buy a small quantity at first and experiment.

do not grow naturally in such a poor soil will be weak and their leaves may show symptoms, but these are variable and diagnosis is not easy. It is best, therefore, unless you intend to grow only those plants which thrive in such a soil, to apply a balanced fertilizer containing major and minor nutrients and trace elements, such as iron, the naturally occurring forms of which are not available on alkaline soils and limestone, and boron and magnesium, both of which are often lacking in sandy soils. On a free-draining soil you will need either to apply a quick-acting fertilizer in small amounts frequently throughout the growing period, or to use a slow-release fertilizer in spring, lightly working it into the surface of the soil. How much you use will depend on the product, but follow the manufacturer's instructions—incorporating too much can actually damage the micro-organisms in the soil and thus your plants. Organic fertilizers such as bonemeal, hoof-and-horn, dried blood and those based on seaweed are on the whole

safer in this respect than manufactured fertilizers. Because your garden is dry and some of your plants grow less rapidly, you may be tempted to give them more fertilizer than normal. This impulse should be resisted. It will result in soft sappy growth and will put plants at risk both from frost and drought.

Plants that actually thrive in drought conditions, such as *Cistus*, rosemary, brooms and those with silver leaves, look and survive better on a meager diet and should not be given much, if any, fertilizer. Wild flowers abhor fertilizer. Grouping or zoning plants according to their nutritional requirements makes good sense (see page 31).

Drainage

A discussion of drainage in a book about dry gardens may be unexpected but while the movement of water through the soil should be slow, it must be continuous so that air is drawn in behind it. If the drainage is inadequate, the soil becomes waterlogged, air is excluded and the roots of most plants die.

Water must also reach plant roots. In unimproved clay soils water will only penetrate to one third of the depth that the same amount reaches in a sandy soil. Digging over clay soil in the autumn and leaving the ground rough to expose as large a surface as possible to frost action will improve its drainage. At the same time you could incorporate some gypsum or, if you wish to raise the pH, lime. These combined treatments will cause the tiny clay particles to group together into crumbs, like those in a loaf of bread, opening up the soil and improving drainage.

All sorts of soil can suffer from compaction which impedes drainage. This can be the result of heavy construction machinery running over the land, particularly in wet weather, and is a problem often found around new houses. Very badly compacted ground will require deep digging.

Similar to compacted soil is a hardpan—an almost impervious layer of soil. Hardpans can occur where land is cultivated mechanically to the same depth every year, but they can also have a mineral origin, for instance in soils with a high iron content. Fortunately, once they are broken up by deep digging, hardpans take many years to reform.

Planting the dry garden

The best time to plant the dry garden will depend on the climate in your area, but the basic plan should be to give trees, shrubs and hardy perennials as long as possible to establish before they are subjected to the worst extremes of the weather. If your winters are mild, then plant in the autumn or early winter; should winter be the rainy season and summer hot and dry, then you will certainly want to get your plants in as soon as cooler weather arrives in autumn. If you live where winters are severe with lengthy periods of hard frost and snow, then planting should be delayed until spring. Vegetables, which have to

Unlike many bulbs the planting period for colchicums—here Colchicum 'The Giant'—is short as they are dormant for only a relatively brief period in late summer. It is important to order early and plant as soon as the bulbs become available.

be sown at the appropriate season depending on kind, and annuals and plants too tender to survive your winter are exceptions to these general rules and the planting of these must wait until the danger of frost is over. Any plants which are on the borderline of hardiness in your particular area should also be left until the spring before being planted. They will then have several months in which to become acclimatized and established before facing a cold winter.

Never plant or sow seeds into a dry soil. Always water it thoroughly first. Summer is the most unsuitable season for planting. If you have no

alternative but to plant then, be prepared to water daily when necessary and to erect temporary shading.

New plants for the dry garden should be young and healthy as these adapt more quickly to their new environment than do large, older and possibly pot-bound specimens, which will also need much more water until they have made new roots.

Preparing the ground

Before undertaking any actual planting clear the ground of all weeds and then dig it over or rotovate it as deeply as you can. You can incorporate compost or manure at this stage. Alternatively you can spread it on the surface to an even depth once the digging is completed, then fork or rotovate it into the cultivated soil. This ensures that the compost is incorporated evenly. The ideal opportunity for this treatment is when replanting a border or large area.

Where you are adding a plant to an existing garden or within a grassy area, dig a hole considerably larger than that needed for the roots. Grass competes strongly for moisture and food, so when planting a tree or shrub in a lawn or rough grass area, remove the turf from a circle at least 4 ft. in diameter. When planting an individual tree or shrub in sandy soil, mix manure or compost to the soil you will return to the hole at the rate of one part manure to two parts soil. If your soil is heavy clay, there is a risk that improved soil will absorb more water than the surrounding soil and become a subterranean bog. To prevent this, you should incorporate several handfuls of sharp, pea-sized grit to the returned soil and use the compost or manure as a mulch around the plant instead.

If yours is a windswept garden, it may be worth spraying the leaves of newly introduced trees and shrubs with an anti-transpirant preparation of the sort used by garden centers to help prevent needle drop in Christmas trees. These sprays combat dehydration by reducing the loss of water through the leaves, but remember that their use can never be a substitute for watering.

Even plants naturally adapted to a dry soil will appreciate a good mulch. This beautifully arranged group consists of the golden Euphorbia polychroma, *a drift of* Lavandula stoechas pendunculata *displaying its long insect-attracting petals, silvery* Senecio cineraria 'White Diamond' *and, in the background, yellow* Phlomis fruticosa. *The rounded shape of these plants is offset by the narrow upright leaves of* Gladiolus communis byzantinus.

Ilex aquifolium

No shrub or tree can surpass for its autumn and winter berries a well-laden specimen of holly. As the fruit ripens it provides a delicious meal for the birds, so to ensure that you have some berried branches left for decorations at Christmas time, it is advisable to try to net a few branches. The small green-yellow flowers are produced in spring, male flowers on one tree, female on another, and both must be present for a good harvest of berries. There are a few hollies, however, which do not require cross-fertilization, including I. aquifolium 'Pyramidalis,' which has the added advantage of a neat upright shape.

Mulches

Strangely, considering its advantages, the practice of regular mulching—applying a layer of traditionally organic material over the surface of the soil—came late to European gardens. Up until 25 years ago, the only plants to be routinely mulched were woodland dwellers like rhododendrons, which stood a good chance of being tucked up with a layer of oak or beech leaves or even pine needles, heathers, which were understood to need peat, and alpines, particularly the more difficult sorts, which were surrounded with fine grit to keep their crowns dry in winter and their roots cool and moist in summer. From time to time, farmyard manure or compost might have been spread around certain crops with the principal aim of feeding them. Lawn mowings were often dumped on rose beds, probably because this was an easy way of disposing of them, and as such was condemned by fastidious gardeners who said it looked untidy. In fact, grass clippings will keep down weeds and enrich the soil as long as the mulch is built up in thin layers, and no mowings from a lawn recently treated with a herbicide are included.

Organic mulches

Mulches composed of organic matter have a limited life span but improve the soil as they decay. Invaluable as soil improvers, farmyard manure and garden compost which are not well made are less than ideal as mulches because they may carry a large crop of weed seeds. Although straw and hay are inexpensive, they may contain weed seeds and, until they begin to rot and darken in color, they are unattractive especially as they are readily blown about. Straw and hay mulches should be spread at least 4 in. thick for protecting plants against frost.

There are plenty of other kinds of sterilized mulches available which reduce weeding and make what has to be done much easier. Loose mulches like bark or coconut shells will not suppress perennial weeds such as docks, bindweed and ground elder. These must be dug out first or treated with an appropriate herbicide but a mulch makes them easier to spot and treat without getting the herbicide on your plants. With a loose mulch a space can easily be cleared for a few seeds or small plants, the soil being covered again once the plants are large enough or have been removed at the end of the season.

Pulverized conifer bark used as a mulch has a great following and is available in a range of grades. The largest grade—variously labeled as chips, nuggets or landscape grade—is the most durable, the best at conserving moisture and the least likely to be blown about by the wind. In certain situations, for example around herbaceous plants or covering beds on a terrace, a finer grade is more appropriate. Applied in a layer at least 2 in. thick, pulverized bark should last two years before it needs to be replenished. To protect the roots of a tender plant from frost, a 6 in. layer is necessary.

Rose and other shrub prunings as well as hedge trimmings are easily converted into home-made wood mulch if passed through a compost shredder. Anyone with lots of woody garden waste would do well to invest in such a machine. The resultant mulch will be less attractive than commercial products, but it will save lighting a woodfire, or a trip to the municipal dump. It is advisable to add a sprinkling of sulfate of ammonia or hoof-and-horn to homemade wood mulch when applying it.

Crushed coconut shells, a by-product of chocolate production, can also be used as a mulch. Spread at the same thickness as bark, they contain more nitrogen. They are easy to spread, and once they have taken up moisture the surface of the layer cakes, preventing the fragments from being blown about by the wind. Some gardeners mix the coconut shells with sawdust before applying them.

You may be fortunate to have a local source of organic waste which can be used as a mulch or, if only available in small quantities, added to your compost heap. Bracken fern, spent hops, grape pressings, cotton seed hulls and seaweed are all said to be excellent. The only one of which I have personal experience is spent hops. These make an excellent mulch with a pleasing appearance, although for a few days after applying the garden may smell like a brewery!

There are some other drawbacks to organic mulches. Robins and thrushes scatter bark on to neighboring surfaces as they search for food, making the garden untidy. However, you can overcome this nuisance by pegging down a 6 in. or so strip of netting on the soil along the front edge of the bed before applying the mulch. Coarse mulch materials can smother small plants unless you are careful and can discourage ground-cover plants that spread by producing runners from colonizing. They can attract slugs; mice may take up residence in straw or hay, which may, incidentally, retain herbicide residues which could affect your plants. Some mulching materials can be a fire hazard and those which are easily combustible should not be used adjacent to buildings. While soil under a mulch will be warmer in winter than if it is left uncovered, the air above the mulch will be colder because the heat in the soil will be trapped and unable to escape.

Inorganic mulches

Inorganic mulches, besides those natural materials like shingle and rock which need to be considered as an element of garden design (see pages 28–9), consist of man-made plastic sheeting. Although this will last much longer than an organic mulch and may be better at suppressing weeds, it has few other benefits and the disadvantage of being unattractive.

WHY MULCH?

- Conserves moisture by reducing the amount of water lost from the soil by evaporation.
- Allows rain to soak into the soil more readily than into an unmulched one.
- Supresses weeds.
- Repels heat and cold.
- Maintains a more even temperature around the plant roots.
- Prevents deep penetration of frosts.
- On a slope protects the soil from erosion.

Commercial growers have used heavy-duty black polyethylene sheeting for many years as an inexpensive way of suppressing weed growth and reducing the need for watering. Spread it on the ground between the plants and punch small holes into it using a garden fork to allow water and a certain amount of air to reach the soil. You can disguise the unattractive appearance of the sheeting by covering it with a thin layer of soil or bark chips.

Spun polypropylene sheeting is more expensive than polyethylene but is manufactured for the task in hand. It allows air, water and dissolved nutrients to pass through the material but because it does not admit light, weeds cannot germinate. Sold in rolls, it can be cut to fit around existing plants; if you are planting a new area, it can be placed on the soil first and slits made in it with a sharp spade for planting. The edges are fixed with pegs and pushed into the soil. A covering of organic mulch will improve its appearance and increase its life.

Excellent for weed control and water conservation, sheeting does have some drawbacks. Applying a granular fertilizer is not possible once the sheet is in place, so if feeding is necessary, you will have to use a foliar feed. Every time you wish to add a new plant or adjust your original planting you have to cut a new hole. And putting in a group of annuals or bedding plants is more difficult.

A mulch of crushed stone is excellent where an arid desert effect is deemed appropriate. It can be more dramatic still if larger pieces of the same rock can be made to appear as if they have been exposed by the action of natural forces. This restrained planting consists of the tender Yucca aloifolia 'Variegata' and pink scabious.

Crushed coconut shells produce a mulch which both conserves moisture and discourages weed growth. It also has an attractive appearance, especially when seen in association with gold-leaved or variegated foliage such as the Hedera helix 'Stift Neuberg' shown here.

Maintaining the dry garden

There is no such thing as a maintenance-free garden. Even a so-called wild or natural garden has to be controlled if nature is not to achieve her desire of returning all cleared land in temperate regions to scrub land and eventually forest. In gardens that are clearly the work of man, lawns and hedges must be cut, weeds removed, mulches supplemented, shrubs pruned, young plants watered, climbers secured, pests and diseases controlled, fertilizers applied, paths and terraces swept—the list at times seems endless. But not all tasks are equally urgent; some like pruning, hedge trimming and the removal of the dead growth of herbaceous plants and annuals can be spread over several weeks, but if you postpone dealing with weeds, pests and diseases and lawn mowing you may well end up with even more work.

Weeds

Weed control is important in every garden but doubly so in the dry garden; not only do weeds encroach on the plants and look unattractive but they steal precious water. It is impossible to rid a garden entirely of weeds but by using mulches wherever possible (see pages 41–3) you will have far fewer to deal with, and by removing those that do grow while they are small and before they have seeded you will save hours of hard work later.

Weeds on sandy soils are relatively easy to deal with by hand but they also germinate much more freely, even when the days are still short. Fortunately, walking on a light soil or working it soon after rain does no damage, so we do not have to call a truce in the battle against weeds in winter.

Used with the utmost care, chemical herbicides can be of enormous help, particularly when overgrown land may have to be cleared. In established gardens herbicides, with the exception of those used for lawns or paths, can be restricted to occasions when, for instance, bindweed is seen climbing a favorite shrub, or a dock has invaded a patch of thyme. It should be possible to paint the leaves of the weed with a herbicide containing glyphosate, without harming the ornamental plant.

Pre-emergent herbicides are incorporated into the soil surface where they kill weeds as they germinate. They require great care in handling and the manufacturer's instructions must be followed. Also, they are not safe to use with all plants. For these reasons I make no use of them in my own garden.

Pests and diseases

Although the dry garden is no more subject to pests and diseases than any other, when plants are put under stress as they are when short of water, they are more vulnerable. It pays, therefore, to be particularly vigilant during dry spells and to try to control the pest or disease as soon as it appears and before it can spread. If chemical measures are necessary, concentrate your watering on the affected plants.

Caring for lawns

A good lawn needs every bit as much care and attention and money lavished on it as any other part of the garden, but too often it fails to get it, and it is usually the first part of the garden to suffer from lack of water, although a lawn that has burned brown normally recovers as soon as conditions improve. If you are determined to keep your lawn green throughout a dry period, then you will have to irrigate it (see pages 46–51), but grass that is deeply rooted and healthy will be much better at withstanding the effects of drought.

Most of us allow our grass to get too long and then cut it too short. Experts seem to agree that not more than one-third of a grass blade should be removed at each mowing and that by keeping a lawn at a reasonable height not only will the longer grass help shade the roots from the hot sun but those roots will be more extensive.

As well as receiving regular applications of fertilizer to replace the nutrients removed by mowing, the lawn needs to be scarified, spiked and top-dressed in autumn or spring, using a mixture of soil, sand and well-rotted compost or manure in equal parts (see "Maintaining a lawn," right). Scarification consists of raking out the thatch of old, tangled grass stems that form at the base of turf and prevent water from reaching the grass roots, while spiking gets water and air even further into the soil and encourages deep rooting. Spiking can be done with solid tines or with hollow ones that actually extract a core of soil. The purpose of top-dressing is to improve the level of the lawn and to feed the grasses; it helps if spiking and scarifying have been carried out in advance. On dry, sandy soil, replace the sand in the mixture with more compost. On a clay soil, use more sand and less soil and compost.

If you are making a lawn from scratch, it is sensible to get it off to a good start. Obtain either a grass seed mixture that is formulated for both your soil and climate (ask your supplier) or a turf grown from such seed. Prepare the seedbed thoroughly. Break up any compaction and hardpan and make sure there is no buried rubble or old foundations. Check that drainage is adequate; on a clay soil it may be necessary to put in a drainage system taking the water to a ditch or soakaway. Incorporate some organic matter if your soil is light and sandy. While the surface of the lawn need not be a true level, any slope should be even. The important thing is not to have any hollows or high spots, as water will collect in one and run off the other.

Although thirsty and demanding of time and money, there is nothing like a well-maintained lawn for providing a foreground to a beautiful mixed border. Here, yellow Laburnum *and pale mauve* Wisteria *form a colorful backdrop to a border of gray-leaved* Brachyglottis, *purplish-leaved* Hebe *'Mrs Winder' and the strong foliage of* Helleborus argutifolius. *Between these* Allium aflatunense *thrust their purple heads into the sun. The exuberant planting is steadied by balls of clipped box.*

Maintaining a lawn

Scarification allows water to reach the roots of the grass. An ordinary garden springbok rake can be used for scarifying and a garden fork for spiking small lawns, but if you have a lot of grass to maintain, it will be worth buying or hiring a powered machine. For most lawns, top-dressing consists of spreading a mixture of soil, sand and well-rotted compost or manure in equal parts as a thin layer over the grass and then working it down toward the roots with the back of a garden rake or a besom broom, as illustrated here.

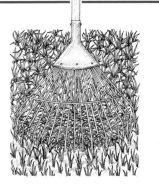

Scarification
Rake the lawn surface vigorously to pull up the thatch and dead grass.

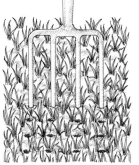

Spiking
Insert a fork in the lawn, then pull it back slightly to let in more air.

Top-dressing
Work the top-dressing down toward the roots using a besom broom.

The role of irrigation

Improving the soil so that it will conserve water, mulching the surface to reduce evaporation and choosing the right plants (see pages 53–97) will ensure that watering can be reduced and on some soils eliminated altogether.

For those who live in cool, normally damp climes or where rainfall is usually sufficient to replace the moisture which is continuously being lost by evaporation, watering will be necessary only during the occasional heat wave or prolonged drought. Where rain is totally lacking for months on end and hot sun bakes the ground, then irrigation becomes a way of life, unless it has been decided to make a garden using only plants that need no extra water. But even those plants, most of which will doubtless be natives, need additional water until they are established and can fend for themselves. Wherever we live, however, it is becoming increasingly important to use water effectively and only when needed.

The ground rules

The first golden rule of watering is not to start before it is necessary. Plants should be encouraged to send their roots deep into the soil; if watering begins too early in the season, there is no inducement for them to do so and they will suffer later when the surface soil begins to dry out. Some trees, shrubs and plants, however, are naturally shallow-rooting, the classic examples being rhododendrons, azaleas and hydrangeas, and they cannot be made to change character, although they do seem capable of some adaptation. In exceptionally hot, dry summers, such shallow-rooting plants growing in normally moist and more humid conditions will suffer more than those growing in naturally drier areas.

The second rule is that while sufficient water should be given to penetrate beyond the root system of the plant you are watering, you should water as infrequently as your soil permits. Clay is able to absorb more water than sand but at a slower rate, and will retain it longer. Because of this, clay soils need to be given more water at a slower rate at each application and the applications can be widely spaced. Sandy soil, by contrast, has to be watered more frequently but needs to be given less water and at a quicker rate (see pages 34–5).

The best time of day to water is early in the morning so that your plants will have moisture just when they need it most. If this is not possible, then the evening is the best alternative. Watering at midday, particularly on very hot, sunny days, is a waste of water and should be avoided at all costs.

The process of transpiration

If a plant wilts during the day but looks perfectly healthy at night, it is a sign that the root system is inadequate and unable to replace the water that is being lost through the leaves by evaporation. Plants extract water from the soil and expel it through tiny breathing pores in their leaves which are open during the day but closed at night. In order to prevent such plants from wilting, it is necessary to create shade and shelter and spray the leaves with water, thus increasing the surrounding level of humidity.

During the process of transpiration water and nutrients are drawn up from the roots and water is lost through breathing pores in the leaf.

When to water

It is not always easy to determine when watering is essential. If you know your plants well, you may be able to recognize the signs. In some cases there will be a lack of growth, leaves may droop or take on subtle changes of color, eventually they will wilt. If the wilting occurs during the day but the plant recovers at night, it is not due to lack of water but to a process known as transpiration, which is the continual water loss from a plant through its leaves (see "The process of transpiration," below left).

If water is in short supply or you have only a limited amount of time for gardening, concentrate your watering on those plants that really need it. This includes anything which has not yet had time to make a good root system. Recently planted trees and shrubs in particular require pampering. Many of them will very probably have been grown in rather soft conditions—plenty of moisture, shelter and food—in order to achieve the largest possible plant in the shortest possible time. Adapting to conditions in your garden will take time. Judicious pruning to reduce the amount of leaf they are carrying, temporary shading and protection from wind will all lessen their need for water.

By the end of the first year most woody subjects should be established but trees purchased as bare root standards 8 ft. or more tall often need regular watering during the second and even third years. To ensure that water reaches the root zone of trees, it is worth sinking a length of plastic drainpipe, drilled with holes, vertically into the soil beside the tree. You can prevent the holes becoming blocked with soil by surrounding the pipe with gravel. Alternatively, fill the pipe with gravel, although this will reduce the amount of water it can receive in one go.

Half-hardy bedding plants are another group of plants particularly at risk. Because they cannot be planted out until the danger of frost is over, they have little time to make roots before hot, dry weather arrives. When it does, irrigate until you judge that they are established and then gradually extend the periods between watering.

A lawn suffering from a shortage of water is easy to spot; growth stops, its bright color dulls to a gray-green and the blades of grass fail to spring back after being trodden on. If you intend to water your lawn through a dry period, this is the time to start; if you wait until it turns brown, it will be much more difficult to get water to soak in and recovery will take much longer. But do not irrigate every day and never give just a light sprinkling. Water thoroughly and then, depending on the temperature and soil type, wait several days before applying more.

How much water your lawn needs to keep it green is an impossible question to answer because it all depends on the type of grass you are growing, the hours of sunshine it receives, your microclimate and the soil type of your garden. However, authorities

Daylilies, such as this Hemerocallis minor, will thrive in any soil except the very driest. However, they will flower more freely and for longer if they are watered from the time their first buds are visible until the last blooms are over.

seem to be agreed that ½ in. of water applied every four days is about right. To find out how long it takes your sprinkler to deliver this amount, place several identical straight-sided containers around the lawn and run the sprinkler until the average depth of water in them is ½ in.

If you are new to gardening, however, it is safer to check on your soil rather than on your plants to find out if you need to water and, when you have done so, if you have given enough. The easiest, and the cheapest, way to find out about the moisture of your soil is to dig a small hole about 10 in. deep and actually feel the soil around it. If it is not noticeably moist, then it is time to start watering.

A soil auger or probe is designed to extract a plug of soil so that its texture, depth of topsoil and so on can be ascertained. It can also be used to check on moisture content, not only before watering but afterward as well, enabling you to make sure you are giving enough water. For instance, if you extract a sample the day after watering and find that only the top 4 in. of soil are moist whereas the water needs to penetrate to 8 in. to reach roots, then you know that it will be necessary to water for twice as long. When taking samples remember that soil dries out from the surface downward.

A tensiometer is used for measuring the amount of moisture in the soil. It consists of a tube, which you push into the ground, with a meter at the top from which to take readings. Some tensiometers are portable so that measurements can be taken any-where in the garden and at varying depths; others are intended to be fixed permanently and usually form part of an automatic watering system.

Once you have decided that it is time to start watering, there is no need to give all your plants the same amount. If plants naturally adapted to a dry environment receive copious watering, they may produce plenty of leaf but not much flower, examples being nasturtiums and pelargoniums.

Conversely, many old favorites of the herbaceous border, including delphiniums, phlox, Michaelmas daisies, campanulas, *Thalictrum* and *Physostegia*, must never be short of moisture if they are to give of their best and produce beautiful blooms. They certainly are not plants for very dry conditions.

Methods of watering

Although hostas need moisture at all times, they will thrive in the dry garden provided they are given shade, shelter, a soil enriched with manure or compost and a good mulch. In addition, by watering them during periods of drought they will respond with larger leaves and more flowers. Here, gold-edged Hosta fortunei *var.* aureomarginata *is growing well in a mixed border of shrubs and climbers.*

Essentially, there are three ways to irrigate: by hand, using a watering can or a hose; from a sprinkler or some other device fitted to the end of the hose; or by installing a permanent or semi-permanent system which may be controlled manually or electronically. Each has its advantage but also some drawbacks. In many countries it is now a legal requirement to fit a back siphonage protection device between a hose and the house water supply. The purpose of this device is to ensure that water supplies are not contaminated by foul water, chemicals or the like being sucked back up the hose, which is a possibility if the water pressure drops.

Watering by hand

A watering can enables the gardener to direct a measured quantity of water accurately just where it is needed, which is to the roots of the plant, either in a gentle flow or, in the case of seedlings, in a fine spray. Watering the bare soil between plants can be avoided, which will save water and discourage weeds. But water is heavy to carry and hand-watering in any quantity is tiring and time-consuming.

A hose connected to a tap or standpipe enables you to give individual plants or small areas a good soaking and to assess the amount of water being applied, but hauling a long hose about is not the most enjoyable of tasks. It is all too easy to pull it across a flower bed and decapitate some favorite plants. Placing temporary metal rods or stout canes at strategic points around which you can pull the hose will help prevent this. Life is also made easier if you fit a spray nozzle, complete with a trigger for controlling the flow, on the end of your hose.

Using a sprinkler

Sprinkler systems, whether movable as described here or as part of a more permanent system (see page 50), are effective for watering the lawn or any major part of the garden, although they are wasteful of water as much evaporates before reaching the plants. Available in a variety of forms (see "Garden sprinklers," below), the cheapest is a nozzle on top of a spike. At the other end of the scale, and price range, are pulse-jet sprinklers, sometimes known as rain guns. Somewhat less expensive are oscillating sprinklers. Both the pulse-jet and oscillating sprinklers need good water pressure.

When choosing a sprinkler, try to match its distribution pattern to the shape you need to cover and, remember, if it only waters a limited area, you will have to move it more often. For a clay soil, select a model which waters slowly; if you buy one which puts out a great volume, you may get puddles forming or have to suspend operations until the water has had time to soak in.

Garden sprinklers

Static garden sprinklers, suitable only for a small lawn, have no moving parts and comprise a nozzle on top of a spike, which is pushed into the ground and the water is thrown out in a circular pattern. Pulse-jet sprinklers produce a single jet which rotates in a series of bursts, sending the water in a circular pattern to cover a large area but at a slow rate. Oscillating sprinklers have a perforated tube which moves back and forth, so that the spray covers a rectangular area. The rate of application is moderate.

Static sprinkler

Pulse-jet sprinkler

Oscillating sprinkler

It is possible to fit a timing device which, after a predetermined period, will turn off the water between your garden tap and the hose connected to your sprinkler. Another device will turn off the water after a selected volume has been applied and electronically operated timers can be programmed to activate the sprinkler over a two-week period.

Irrigation systems

For those parts of the garden where a gentle spray or trickle of water is preferable, there are leaky hoses that either have rows of tiny holes along their entire length or are porous so that water escapes over the whole surface (see "Methods of irrigation," below).

From a buried perforated hose, it is only a small step to a semi-permanent, drip-irrigation system which may be controlled manually or electronically. The system consists of a rigid or flexible supply tube with a number of side branches (see "Methods of irrigation," below). These are laid on the surface of the soil where they can be hidden by a mulch. Water trickles from a nozzle known as an emitter. Instead of ordinary drip emitters, mini-sprinklers and misters can be fitted to distribute water over a larger area. This sort of system can be connected to the mains but because it works under low pressure, it may need a pressure regulator fitted as well as a filter. Trickle irrigation uses water very economically and can be rerouted when necessary but it has two drawbacks.

The tiny outlets tend to get blocked and need regular cleaning, while a network of pipes lying on the surface can easily be dislodged.

A permanent system of irrigation employs sprinklers working under complex controls. A grid of buried pipes supplies a series of sprinklers; those for watering lawns normally sit just below the grass but under pressure pop up and send out a strong circular or sectional spray. Nozzles for watering the rest of the garden are fixed permanently above ground level. This method of irrigation works under high pressure and may require a pressurizing pump. Careful advance planning is essential and installation is best entrusted to an expert. A well-programmed installation will be connected to a moisture sensor so that watering will only take place when the soil is dry. A "rain shut off" control will prevent the system working during or soon after rain has fallen.

Undoubtedly, an efficient, automatic watering system makes the most effective use of water. Assuming that water authorities are able to meet the increasing demand, there is no doubt that many more gardeners will wish to install full irrigation in the future. It will be a pity, however, if the special character of the dry garden is lost so that it becomes like any other garden. My hope is that irrigation will be used with restraint and that we will accept our soils and our climate in order to grow that special range of plants which have adapted to them.

Methods of irrigation

A leaky hose with holes can be laid with the perforation uppermost or turned upside down so that a narrow strip of soil is soaked. Porous (soaker) hoses are best buried just below the surface to ensure the tubing remains moist, so that calcium in the water is less likely to clog the pores. In a drip-irrigation system thin "spaghetti" tubing can be inserted anywhere along the supply lines to take water to an individual plant. All these systems direct water where it is needed and so are preferred to sprinklers, which tend to waste water.

A leaky hose with its holes facing upward produces a fine spray for watering plants in rows.

Porous hoses allow water to seep slowly into the soil and are ideal for newly planted beds.

"Spaghetti" tubing takes water to plants without disturbing the soil around the roots.

In countries with long, hot, dry summers, an expanse of verdant green grass, which can only be achieved by pouring vast quantities of water on to it, can either be regarded as a refreshing oasis in a parched desert or an inappropriate intrusion into a landscape which is otherwise brown and sear. Where a lawn is deemed essential, it is even more important that the other plants in the garden should be able to survive with only an occasional soaking, as is the case with the pink Nerium oleander, *the scented* Trachelospermum *on the pergola, the lavender and the clipped box edging the well-manicured lawn.*

PLANTS FOR THE
DRY GARDEN

The most intriguing and enjoyable part of creating a successful garden comes with choosing the right plants, and this means not only selecting those that are suitable for the climate and soil, but also the ones that successfully fulfill a specific need. This might be screening an eyesore, creating shade or shelter, or performing a design function by providing a certain color, texture or shape. Above all, you will want to choose plants that will give you pleasure with their flowers, fruit, beautiful foliage or wonderful scent.

In Beth Chatto's garden, southeastern England in late autumn, the platelike heads of Sedum spectabile 'Brilliant' contrast with the miniature spires of Kniphofia 'Little Maid,' while Caryopteris × clandonensis 'Kew Blue' provides complementary color. Behind the seat Lavatera 'Barnsley' is still full of flower; in front of it tussocks of Stipa tenuissima resemble exploding fireworks, and to the left Sedum telephium maximum 'Atropurpureum' rises from silvery Artemisia stelleriana.

How plants resist drought

Assembling a list of plants that will grow in dry conditions is not quite as straightforward as it might seem, for drought-resistance is a relative term. Some plants can survive on remarkably small amounts of water, others are slightly drought-tolerant and may need more moisture than your climate and soil can provide. Most silver-leaved plants and conifers like junipers, for example, must have very well drained soils and so are useless if your soil is heavy clay, which is dry in summer but lies wet in winter. Others, like hardy geraniums, *Alchemilla* and many flowering shrubs, are more adaptable. It is all a question of matching your conditions with the plants' needs, and as those needs have only been measured scientifically in a very minor way in ornamental plants, we have to rely on our own and others' observations. However, it does help in making a choice to have some knowledge of the various means by which plants have adapted to a shortage of water.

Hollyhocks (Alcea), *whose tall spires of saucer-shaped flowers never look better than when growing against a cottage wall, make long tap roots in order to find moisture deep in the soil.*

Root systems

Some trees send out a dense system of roots in all directions so as to extract all the available moisture over a wide area. Such trees, and they include birches and cherries as well as large kinds like some maples and *Ailanthus*, are able to withstand considerable drought, at least in cool climates, but their hungry, questing roots make it difficult to grow other plants within their root zone. This is not such a problem when starting with a young sapling as the surrounding plants will have time to become established.

Many plants send their roots deep into the soil in order to tap moisture which is not available near the surface. Three plant families have made a speciality of this sort of root system. They are the Papaveraceae which includes, besides the true poppies, the Californian poppy *(Eschscholzia)* and Californian tree poppy *(Romneya)*, the Umbelliferae, sometimes known as the carrot family of which *Eryngium* (sea holly) is a member, and the Leguminosae. This last group includes such important food crops as peas and beans, trees like *Robinia* and *Gleditsia*, shrubs which include *Acacia*, *Cercis*, *Colutea*, *Coronilla*, *Indigofera*, laburnum, lupin and all the brooms. The legumes can also extract nitrogen—the essential plant food——from the atmosphere and storing it in their roots. This unusual method of producing their own fertilizer makes it possible for them to grow in soils which are nutritionally very deficient.

From the gardener's point of view, a deep tap root is a mixed blessing. It may make the establishment of a desirable plant difficult or limit the size at which it can be moved, so you must be sure when you plant it that you have chosen the right place. Where it belongs to a weed or an ornamental which has sown itself into the wrong place, it can make removal extremely problematic, as anyone coping with the seedlings of fennel *(Foeniculum vulgare)* or Welsh poppy *(Meconopsis cambrica)* will testify. It is no surprise to find that the gound elder, whose invasive roots are so difficult to eradicate, is in the Umbelliferae family.

Other plants cope with rocky conditions, their sinuous roots penetrating deep into cracks and crevices, following narrow seams of soil which provide a little moisture and humus. *Cistus*, rosemary, sage *(Salvia)*, rue *(Ruta)* and other natives of rocky Mediterranean hillsides have such roots.

Some plants overcome a period of drought by storing water in plump, fleshy roots. Daylilies *(Hemerocallis)*, lily turf *(Liriope)*, *Agapanthus* and red hot pokers *(Kniphofia)* all have roots of this type.

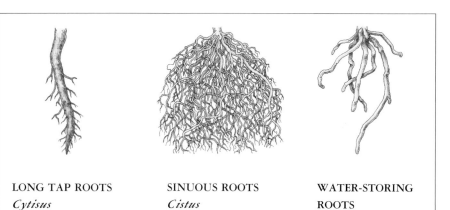

LONG TAP ROOTS	SINUOUS ROOTS	WATER-STORING ROOTS
Cytisus	*Cistus*	*Agapanthus*
Eryngium	*Lavandula*	*Eremurus*
Indigofera	*Phlox subulata*	*Hemerocallis*
Lupinus	*Ruta*	*Kniphofia*
Papaver	*Salvia*	*Liriope*
Romneya	*Tamarix*	

ABOVE *These illustrations show the different types of root system that thrive in dry soils. Examples of plants with such root systems accompany each illustration.*

LEFT *Although the plump white roots of Agapanthus store water, plants will need a rich soil and watering until established in order to survive a drought during the flowering season.*

Some plants have almost dispensed with leaves in order to reduce the amount of moisture that they lose through transpiration. Others, such as this Eschscholzia californica, *have developed filigree leaves.*

Foliage

Leaves give an excellent indication of how plants may be expected to cope with drought, although, of course, there are exceptions to this rule. Large, soft, smooth leaves like those of hostas, primulas and *Ligularia* suggest they need plenty of moisture and shelter as, indeed, they do, whereas the thin needles of pines, the scale-like foliage of junipers and the hard leathery leaves of *Arbutus*, *Elaeagnus* and *Pittosporum* immediately indicate a probable ability to withstand sun, wind and drought. A shiny surface means that a coating of salt will wash off, which is, doubtless, one of the reasons why so many shrubs with glossy foliage make good coastal residents.

A small leaf has less surface area from which moisture can transpire, so it is not surprising that many herbaceous plants and annuals as well as trees and shrubs which have adapted to growing on dry soils have narrow or filigree-like leaves. *Anthemis*, *Armeria*, *Gazania* and blazing star *(Liatris)* all have narrow leaves, while those of *Achillea*, the Californian poppy *(Eschscholzia)* and *Artemisia absinthium* are so deeply indented as to appear almost feathery.

A dense covering of fine hairs protects the leaf surface from sun, wind and salt and at the same time traps drops of moisture from the dew or passing showers. In plants like *Convolvulus cneorum*, *Stachys* and *Artemisia*, the hairs are so pale and the covering

so dense that their leaves appear gray or silver. A smaller number of plants have evolved a protective wax coating which gives them a bluish appearance as can be seen in eucalyptus, rue and *Othonna cheirifolia*. A further strange development has given the leaves of some eucalyptus the ability to turn edgeways onto the sun so that the largest surface is not exposed to the full effect of its rays.

In cacti and succulents, leaves and stems have become thick and fleshy and filled with sap that stores water. The succulents we see most often in cool gardens are sedums and houseleeks *(Sempervivum)* as well as *Portulaca*, *Calandrinia* and *Mesembryanthemum* when grown as half-hardy annuals.

Dormant periods

Another strategy for coping with dry periods is to avoid it altogether. Bulbs lie dormant for months until, with the arrival of rain, they rapidly produce flowers and seed while their leaves manufacture the nutrients which will be stored until the next year. Many plants native to lands with hot, dry summers simply "close up shop" in a severe drought. Perennial grasses, for example, make rapid growth, with the arrival of warmth in spring, in some cases producing their seeds within a few weeks, but as the weather becomes hotter and the soil loses its moisture, they turn brown and apparently lifeless, only to green up and start into growth again with the return of cooler and damper weather in autumn.

Annuals must germinate from seed, grow, flower and set seed all during the period when the soil contains sufficient water, after which the seeds lie dormant until sufficient rain falls again. This ability to germinate and flower quickly can be put to good use in the dry garden (see page 94).

Natural habitats

A plant's origin is another clue to its likely ability to survive on a small amount of water. There is a risk, however, of equating drought with heat and looking only to countries with warm climates for dry garden plants. For those of us who live in colder climates most of the vegetation of warm countries, unless it comes from high altitudes, will not be sufficiently hardy; even those plants from the Mediterranean like

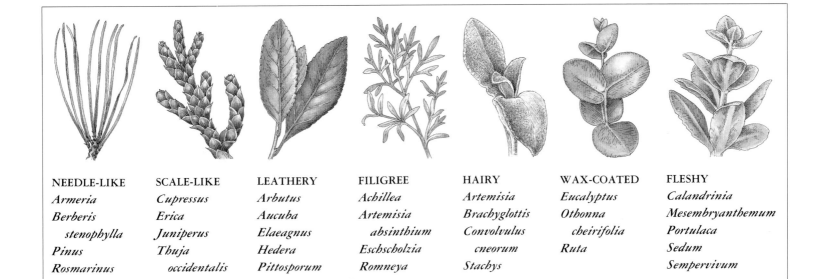

NEEDLE-LIKE	SCALE-LIKE	LEATHERY	FILIGREE	HAIRY	WAX-COATED	FLESHY
Armeria	*Cupressus*	*Arbutus*	*Achillea*	*Artemisia*	*Eucalyptus*	*Calandrinia*
Berberis	*Erica*	*Aucuba*	*Artemisia*	*Brachyglottis*	*Othonna*	*Mesembryanthemum*
stenophylla	*Juniperus*	*Elaeagnus*	*absinthium*	*Convolvulus*	*cheirifolia*	*Portulaca*
Pinus	*Thuja*	*Hedera*	*Eschscholzia*	*cneorum*	*Ruta*	*Sedum*
Rosmarinus	*occidentalis*	*Pittosporum*	*Romneya*	*Stachys*		*Sempervivum*

ABOVE *These illustrations show the different types of foliage that are adept at dealing with drought. Examples of plants with such foliage accompany each illustration.*

RIGHT *A coating of fine hairs protects leaves, stems, even the flower spikes in the case of* Stachys byzantina, *from the worst effects of sun, wind and salt, as well as trapping beads of moisture. Such a dense covering of hairs usually gives the plant a gray or silvery appearance.*

rosemary, holm oak *(Quercus ilex)* and sage, which have been grown in northern Europe for so long that we hardly think of them as foreign can still be damaged or even killed in a severe winter.

Fortunately, a number of warm-climate plants are remarkably tolerant of a wide range of temperatures. Yuccas come mostly from the deserts of Mexico and yet the hardier kinds can withstand severe frost. In their native, sunbaked habitats shrubs like lavender, *Santolina* and rue *(Ruta)*, and herbaceous plants like *Acanthus*, *Agapanthus* and *Cynara*, do not have to contend with more than a few degrees of frost and yet have proved to be surprisingly hardy. Some plants like *Artemisia* are potentially able to survive quite low temperatures but only if they are given a soil which is dry in winter as well as summer. Others need plenty of summer heat to ripen their wood, bulb or rhizome as the case may be. The pomegranate *(Punica granatum)* and the chaste tree *(Vitex agnus-castus)* are examples of Mediterranean shrubs which withstand frost as long as their young shoots have been hardened by late summer and autumn sun.

Other, colder climatic regions which are also subject to drought provide a range of plants of varying hardiness suitable for the temperate dry garden. They are principally coastlines, dry mountain slopes, sunny, windswept plains, sandy heathlands and the dry floor of woods and forests.

A border for a coastal garden

All the plants in this border, shown between mid- and late summer, will tolerate salt spray, high winds and dry sandy soils and, once established, will not be onerous to maintain. In such exposed conditions, it pays to plant more closely than normal so the plants afford each other protection. Here, a few pines at the back of the border provide additional shelter. In a coastal garden, a covering of pebbles, graduating from fine shingle in the front of the border to large stones under the shrubs, forms an appropriate mulch. Although designed to take advantage of the milder coastal winters, this border would also be suitable for a warm, sheltered location inland.

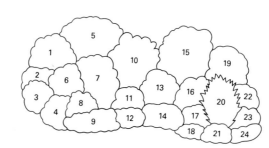

1 *Hebe* 'Midsummer Beauty': evergreen shrubby veronica, 5–6 ft. tall, with long, lavender-purple racemes from mid-summer until autumn; narrow, light green leaves with reddish undersides.

2 *Genista hispanica* (Spanish gorse): a positive hedgehog of a shrub with 2 ft. tall spiny branches smothered in golden-yellow flowers in late spring and early summer.

3 *Kniphofia* 'Little Maid': a red-hot poker but with creamy yellow flowers on 2 ft. stems in late summer and autumn; leaves form grassy clumps; herbaceous perennial.

4 *Artemisia* 'Powis Castle': evergreen foliage shrub with silver-gray, filigree leaves making a 2½ ft. high mound.

5 *Spartium junceum* (Spanish broom): upright deciduous shrub, 9 ft. tall; golden, honey-scented flowers on bright green stems from midsummer to autumn.

6 *Cistus × aguilarii* 'Maculatus': 4 ft. tall evergreen rock rose with rich green, rippled leaves and large, white flowers with crimson blotches from early to midsummer.

7 *Bupleurum fruticosum*: evergreen shrub, 5–6 ft. tall, with leathery, strap-shaped leaves and rounded heads of green-yellow flowers from midsummer to early autumn.

8 *Echinops ritro* (globe thistle): blue, ball-shaped flowerheads on stout 3 ft. stems in late summer; divided, grayish foliage; herbaceous perennial.

9 *Salvia officinalis* 'Purpurascens' (purple-leaved sage): sprawling evergreen shrub, about 2 ft. tall, with spikes of violet flowers in midsummer.

10 *Hippophae rhamnoides* (sea buckthorn): deciduous shrubby tree, growing to 12 ft. or more, with narrow, gray-green leaves; plant both male and female plants together to obtain orange berries in autumn.

11 *Libertia formosa*: narrow, dark green, arching leaves and 2½ ft. tall stems displaying clusters of white flowers in mid-summer; evergreen perennial.

12 *Osteospermum jucundum*: large, mauve-pink, daisy flowers cover these 1 ft. high sprawling plants on and off for most of the summer; slightly tender evergreen perennial.

13 *Escallonia* 'Donard Radiance': erect, 6 ft. tall, evergreen shrub with glossy foliage and rose-red, chalice-shaped flowers in early summer, with a spattering of later blooms.

14 *Artemisia stelleriana*: 1 ft. high mat of silvery white leaves and creamy yellow flowers in late summer; evergreen perennial.

15 *Tamarix ramosissima* 'Rubra': rosy red flowers smother the slender, arching branches of this deciduous shrub in late summer; it will reach a height of 12 ft.

16 *Rosa rugosa* 'Fru Dagmar Hastrup': large, single, pale pink flowers from early summer until autumn, the later flowers mingling with bold, tomato-shaped hips; fresh green, deeply veined foliage; grows to 5 ft.

17 *Eryngium × oliverianum* (sea holly): upright herbaceous perennial, growing to a height of

2½ ft., with rounded heads of gray, thimble-like flowers on metallic blue, spiky ruffs produced in late summer.

18 *Erigeron glaucus* (fleabane): the mat-forming, gray-green foliage of this evergreen perennial is covered in summer with pinky mauve daisies on 1 ft. stems.

19 *Olearia × macrodonta*: evergreen shrub capable of reaching 20 ft.; holly-shaped, gray-green leaves with heads of white flowers in early summer.

20 *Phormium tenax* 'Purpureum' (New Zealand flax): shiny, purplish-brown, evergreen, sword-like leaves, 5 ft. long; reddish flowers on 6 ft. tall stems are produced during hot summers.

21 *Hebe* 'Rosie': rounded evergreen shrub, 1½ ft. tall, with small, medium green leaves and many bright pink flowers from midsummer until autumn.

22 *Lycium barbarum*: deciduous shrub, 8 ft. tall, with arching branches and gray-green leaves; funnel-shaped, purple flowers in summer, followed by orange berries.

23 *Lavandula × intermedia* 'Grappenhall': a good form of lavender with gray leaves and blue-purple flowers on long stalks in late summer; evergreen shrub, 3 ft. tall.

24 *Armeria maritima* 'Alba' (thrift): clumps of 4 in. high narrow, dark green leaves and spherical heads of tiny white flowers on stiff stems in late spring and early summer; evergreen perennial.

Framework plants

Plants that are to form the essential structure of the garden need to be effective in winter as well as in summer. Indeed, some, such as this lovely birch Betula ermanii and the yew hedging with its firm lines, can be appreciated even more when the days are shorter and the sun remains low in the sky.

Except in gardens where man-made structures like walls and fences, terraces and paving create the framework, plants are required to provide shelter and privacy, shade and enclosure, define space and carpet the ground. The plants that form the backbone of the garden need to be well adapted to the climate and soil conditions and the more important they are in making the framework, the more certain you should be that you will not lose them through frost or drought. Keep tender, temperamental or short-lived plants for less important positions.

Trees

Slow though they may be to mature, trees are potentially the largest and most permanent of all garden elements and their selection and positioning need more consideration than anything else. Some trees are best as individuals, seen in the foreground against a backdrop of massed trees or buildings. They are also useful for framing views or casting a welcome pool of shade on a lawn or terrace. Their attraction lies in their distinct shape and habit of branching, strong leaf pattern or foliage color. When their form or foliage color is even more unusual and eye-catching, they can be used as focal points in the garden (see pages 80–3).

In large gardens, an outstanding, quick-growing specimen tree for the dry garden with plenty of space is the Tree of Heaven (*Ailanthus altissima*). It can grow to a height of 60 ft. and has luxurious leaves, which can be as much as 3 ft. long, divided into numerous leaflets. The false acacia or black locust (*Robinia pseudoacacia*) is another large tree of rapid growth which eventually reaches a height of about 65 ft. Its leaves make a beautiful pattern and remain a fresh green color all the way through the summer months. Tassles of white pea-like flowers are produced in early summer and the trunk is attractively furrowed and gnarled.

Somewhat similar in general appearance and size to *Robinia pseudoacacia* but free of thorns and suckers is *Sophora japonica*, the pagoda tree from China. I like this tree but you will have to wait about thirty years to see its creamy white flowers and only then in appreciable numbers in a hot summer. The honey locust (*Gleditsia triacanthos*), which is a quick-growing tree reaching a maximum height of 70 ft., belongs to the same family (Leguminosae) as both the *Robinia* and *Sophora* and like them it has attractive frond-like leaves (see page 108).

Deciduous specimen trees for a medium-sized garden include *Koelreuteria* (see page 109) and two species of ash, both of which can reach a height of 33 ft. The Arizona ash (*Fraxinus velutina*), which can withstand cold as well as heat, has another popular name of velvet ash because its young shoots and leaves are covered in gray down. *Fraxinus ornus* is known as the manna or flowering ash because of its large panicles of creamy flowers in late spring and clusters of brown seed pods. The dark green leaves can take on purple tints in the autumn.

My own favorite Japanese cherry is *Prunus* 'Shiro-tae,' whose wide-spreading branches are almost horizontal, producing a level crown of no great height (approximately 13 ft., a distinct advantage where a specimen is needed that will not obscure the view from an upstairs window. In spring large, pure white flowers on long stalks line every branch. While the bark of this cherry is attractive enough, in the taller *P. serrula* (approximately 23 ft.) it is of a quality to outshine all others, the color being a rich mahogany-red, enhanced by a light-reflecting gloss. The leaves are narrower and more distinguished than other cherries but the white flowers are small and largely hidden in the foliage. Oriental cherries are very amenable to all soil types and more suitable for the dry garden than those other favorites of the spring, the ornamental crab apples. However, cherries are unable to withstand prolonged drought when it is combined with heat.

Even a very small garden is usually improved by the addition of a diminutive tree or two. The Judas tree (*Cercis siliquastrum*; see page 108) and oleaster or Russian olive (*Elaeagnus angustifolia*; see page 113) are shrubs which grow to tree-like proportions. *Crataegus tanacetifolia*; a slow-growing thorn or May tree, which eventually reaches a height of about 26 ft., bears tiny yellow fruit in autumn. Its gray, downy leaves are so deeply cut that they have earned the tree its common name of tansy-leaved thorn.

The 20 ft. tall silk tree (*Albizia julibrissin* 'Rosea') is excellent for a sunny city garden or where a tropical look is appropriate. Its fern-like leaves have the ability to fold up at night and the late-summer flowers are like clusters of tiny, deep-rose-colored powder puffs. Able to survive cold winter and sea winds, it needs a sandy or gravelly soil and plenty of sun to ripen the wood.

Although in temperate regions most trees are deciduous, there are a number of evergreens suitable for garden specimens but their drawback is that they take years to outgrow their initial shrub-like appearance. *Magnolia grandiflora*, so frequently seen as a huge and, at times, rather ungainly tree, will make

an impressive smaller tree about 26 ft. tall, if a clonal selection, such as 'Brackens Brown Beauty,' is used. The leaves, on this particular selection, are leathery, lustrous and dark green above and a rusty brown color beneath.

The Chinese privet (*Ligustrum lucidum*) makes a most handsome, small rounded tree, about 26 ft. tall, and being deeply rooted it does not rob the soil. The glossy dark green leaves are larger than those of the common privet, while the white flowers in large panicles appear in late summer or autumn when blossoms are at a premium. Unfortunately, it is not a plant for very cold districts.

It is to conifers, however, that we must look for really hardy evergreen trees. When something irregular and striking in appearance is required, try the Hollywood juniper (*Juniperus chinensis* 'Kaizuka'; see page 109). When a massive evergreen tree is required there is nothing more impressive than a cedar (*Cedrus*), but do not expect quick results.

The Judas tree (Cercis siliquastrum), *pictured here in its eastern Mediterranean homeland, is excellent for gardens of practically any size as long as they are well drained and sunny. According to tradition,* Cercis *is the tree from which Judas Iscariot hanged himself, but it normally makes only a small bushy tree whose branches would not support a man's weight.*

Grouping of trees

Some trees look better when they are grouped rather than when planted in isolation. A cluster of three, five or seven silver birch trees need not take up much space if the distance between individuals varies between 2 ft. and 6 ft. Two young saplings can even be planted into the same hole to achieve the multi-stemmed effect which so often occurs in the wild. *Betula ermanii* and *B. jacquemontii* both have superb white bark, while that of *B. albosinensis septentrionalis* is fawn-pink and red, but none of them has the grace of *B. pendula* with its drooping branchlets. The so-called Swedish birch (*B. pendula* 'Dalecarlica') also has the added attraction of deeply cut and feathery leaves.

Something of the same effect as a grove of birch can be achieved by close grouping the Alpine snow gum (*Eucalyptus pauciflora niphophila*). Growing at high altitudes, it is perhaps the hardiest eucalyptus commonly available, but it can also take heat and drought. It usually grows about 20 ft. tall and tends to lean, which makes it unsuitable as a lone tree where a more symmetrical appearance is preferable. Although its gray-green leaves are attractive, it is the subtle patchwork of its bark in shades of cream, gray and green that is outstanding.

Trees and shrubs for screening

Often a tree or group of trees will be needed to give privacy or screen an eyesore. Such planting is usually placed on the perimeter of the garden where it should form a quiet, green backdrop or frame for the more decorative and colorful planting within. For this purpose the least suitable plant is one which attracts attention with its unusual form or colored foliage. The ideal screen is one which cannot be seen through for at least a good part of the year and which remains dense from the ground up. Where there is plenty of room, pines, evergreen oaks and deciduous trees with a dense twiggy habit like *Acer campestre* (see page 108) and *Crataegus* (thorn) might be used. More often space will be at a premium and what is needed are trees of narrow upright habit and quick growth that are able to thrive when planted close together. It is not surprising in view of this specification that × *Cupressocyparis leylandii* are so popular; although if

they are not stopped, they will soar to a height of at least 60 ft. However, if clipped at a height of 10–12 ft., they will make an excellent screen.

There are two forms of *Pyrus* with a narrow upright habit and a reasonable rate of growth which can be used on dry soils in temperate regions. 'Beech Hill' is a selection of *Pyrus communis*, the ancestor of our fruiting pears. It grows to a height of approximately 30 ft., has typical pear blossoms in spring and tiny inedible fruit in autumn. The leaves of *Pyrus calleryana* 'Chanticleer' turn red in autumn, holding

Pines are excellent where a tall screen is required, as well as making a good background for colorful plantings such as this combination of gray-leaved Pyrus salicifolia 'Pendula' and Cotinus coggygria 'Rubrifolius.'

on very late; indeed, in some mild winters it is semi-evergreen. The small white flowers, which are produced in quantity in spring with a spasmodic sprinkling later, add to its attractions.

Where a screen does not need to be of great height, evergreen shrubs are a better choice, although they should be planted closer than in a shrub or mixed border—about 3–4 ft. Some of them will indeed make trees of a sort. Where the temperature does not drop much below 20°F (−7°C), the sweet bay (*Laurus nobilis*), which has a naturally dense cone shape, soon makes a thick screen. The Portuguese

OTHER FRAMEWORK
PLANTS
The following trees
are also well suited
to dry gardens.
Acer platanoides
Aesculus californica
Caragana arborescens
Castanea sativa
Ilex × altaclerensis
Ilex aquifolium
Malus hupehensis
Populus alba
Populus tremuloides
Quercus cerris
Quercus rubra
Sorbus aucuparia

laurel *(Prunus lusitanica)* is hardier but slower to get started although it will eventually reach 15 ft. without getting too wide. *Cotoneaster frigidus* 'Cornubia' will make the same height in a fraction of the time, but it is less dense and semi-evergreen. *Cotoneaster lacteus* makes a more solid bush (see page 112). Both cotoneasters will provide a cheering display of red berries.

The best screens of all are made by yew, holly and box when allowed to grow naturally, just as they make the finest hedges when clipped (see page 64). They are adaptable to sun and shade and a wide range

of soil types, although holly seems to do best on one which is neutral or acid. All need excellent drainage but only in cool climates will English yew *(Taxus baccata)* and common box *(Buxus sempervirens)* tolerate a soil which is actually dry. Common holly *(Ilex aquifolium)* is more adaptable in this respect. These evergreens need to be kept permanently moist for the first few years if a reasonable rate of growth is to be achieved, and even then there will be a long wait for a tall screen. It is often better to mix them with faster-growing deciduous subjects, which can be cut out as the more desirable species take over.

A screen can be made from a mixture of shrubs planted closely together, although it may become difficult to control if some potentially very large species are used. This screen includes variegated hollies, a pine, several Cupressus, Rosa glauca, a purple Berberis and junipers by the path.

Hedges

Garden hedges can be divided into those which are clipped into a living wall, in which case the more architectural they appear the better, and the completely informal sort made from roses, brooms and other shrubs of irregular outline which are little more than a shrub border planted more densely. In the case of the latter, you must expect the hedge to be, on average, as wide at the base as it is high. In between are hedges composed of shrubs like *Berberis*, *Ribes* and *Escallonia* which, if pruned immediately after flowering, can be kept dense and of reasonably formal shape without complete loss of flower.

Clipped hedges

The best shrubs for wall-like hedges are those of dense habit, which under the shears take on the sharpness of stone or brick and then retain it for a good time before needing to be cut again. This is why yew, holly and box have always been classic hedging plants. Yew *(Taxus baccata)* grows naturally on chalk and will tolerate a dry soil as long as it contains plenty of humus. It pays to irrigate young plants and to spray the young foliage with clear water after a hot, drying day.

Holly *(Ilex aquifolium* or *Ilex × altaclerensis)* makes a superb impenetrable barrier and when established withstands drought very well. It has one big drawback. You will never manage to clear up all its dead leaves and unless you habitually do all your weeding in stout gloves, a good proportion of their prickles will end up in your fingers! Common box *(Buxus sempervirens)* is the best choice for a formal hedge on a dry soil, especially one with a high pH. It is very hardy, will grow in shade and succeeds by the ocean. There are selected forms available, the most vigorous being 'Handsworthiensis,' which has larger leaves and is more upright in habit.

Pittosporum tenuifolium, with wavy, shiny, pale gray-green leaves, *Griselinia littoralis*, whose oval leaves are almost yellow, and the dark green Japanese spindle tree *(Euonymus japonicus)* all withstand considerable drought and can be clipped into semi-formal evergreen hedges. They are of more rapid growth than box but less hardy.

Informal hedges

Where a strong, rough hedging material is required, for the boundary of a country garden perhaps, field maple *(Acer campestre)*, quickthorn *(Crataegus monogyna)* and myrobalan plum *(Prunus cerasifera)* will all be perfectly happy growing in dry soils, the last being particularly useful on sand. Hornbeam *(Carpinus betulus)* will also grow on light soils as well as on clay and chalk. Provided it is trimmed in late summer, the hornbeam will hold its withered leaves, into winter, making it good for screening.

Compromise hedges

In small gardens there may be a reluctance to give up space for a hedge and yet a wall or aesthetic fence may be too expensive; in this case a "fedge"—a marriage between a fence and a hedge—may be the answer. The fence can be inexpensive chestnut paling, wattle hurdles or chain link. The hedge is composed of ivy, the best kind being the large-leaved *Hedera colchica*, although any hardy variety of

the common English ivy, *H. helix* (see page 113), can be used, planted at about 3 ft. intervals along the base of the fence. In time the ivy will become self-supporting, even if the fence rots, and it can be clipped twice a year to keep it narrow.

Internal hedges

Waist-high intermediate hedges can be useful in the garden for defining an area or strengthening the design. Such hedges are often more impressive when 4–5 ft. wide and composed of two, three, or even four rows of plants instead of the usual single row. Where a formal hedge is required, box without doubt gives the best result, but if you are impatient and are prepared to clip it three times in summer, the honeysuckle *Lonicera nitida* 'Fertilis' with its small box-like leaves and rapid growth can make a good substitute. *Hypericum* 'Hidcote,' almost any *Berberis* of medium height, *Lavandula spica*, *Potentilla* and *Rosmarinus* 'Miss Jessopp's Upright' all make good, but mainly less formal, low hedges.

HEDGES OF
UNUSUAL COLOR
Atriplex halimus:
   silvery-gray
Berberis thunbergii
   'Atropurpurea':
   purplish-red
Berberis thunbergii 'Rose
   Glow': purplish-red,
   variegated with pink
Cupressus glabra
   'Conica': silvery-blue
Cupressus macrocarpa
   'Goldcrest': yellow
Lonicera nitida
   'Baggesen's Gold':
   golden-yellow, variegated
Prunus cerasifera
   'Nigra': brown-red
Tamarix gallica:
   gray-green

LEFT *Although the best shrubs for creating the permanent framework of the garden are evergreen, there are a few deciduous kinds which are so dense and twiggy or tree-like that they are almost as effective. One such shrub is the silver-leaved* Elaeagnus angustifolia *which, even in winter, is striking for its older wood which has been likened to polished walnut, and the contrasting young shoots covered in silvery scales. The strange topiary creature has been created from yew.*

Structural plants

Even a small garden or one which sets out to appear naturalistic needs some plants that will accentuate views and provide a mainly green background for more colorful plants. The majority need to be evergreen and if they provide flowers or berries during the months when the foreground plants are resting, so much the better.

Viburnum tinus (see page 117) is the ideal background shrub, with demure clusters of pink or white flowers when the opulent beauties to which it played second fiddle have been consigned to the compost heap. *Pyracantha*, the taller cotoneasters and *Aucuba* all make good background plants and their berries provide color and food for the birds in the shortening days of autumn. In early spring *Berberis* and *Osmanthus* × *burkwoodii* add a bonus of flowers to the year-round benefit of their glossy foliage.

Among the tall evergreen *Berberis* are the orange-flowered *B. darwinii* with very dark green leaves and the less prickly *B.* × *stenophylla* with pleasantly arching branches bespangled in spring with small yellow flowers. The plain-leaved aucubas are undeniably handsome, the female plants producing large scarlet berries. *Aucuba japonica* 'Salicifolia,' with long, narrow and slightly jagged leaves, is particularly distinguished and is female, but to produce berries it must be near a male *A. japonica*.

Osmanthus × *burkwoodii* and Japanese privet (*Ligustrum japonicum*) are both upright, becoming rounded later, and have leathery, olive-green leaves making them a good foil to other plants. They both produce white flowers, those of the *Osmanthus* being freely borne in spring and sweetly scented while those of the privet come in later summer with only a slight fragrance. The mature leaves of *Photinia* × *fraseri* 'Red Robin' are large, dark green and glossy but on opening they are bright red and only slowly pass to copper and eventually green. The young shoots are easily damaged by frost and as growth starts so early in the year this shrub should be positioned out of the rays of the early-morning sun.

In gardens which do not suffer from cold winds or hard frosts, the more tender evergreens such as the strawberry tree (*Arbutus unedo*), more often seen as a

ABOVE RIGHT *The laurustinus, of which this* Viburnum tinus *'Gwenllian' is an improved form, makes a good informal hedge and is a most dependable evergreen shrubs for building up the shape of the garden. Flowering begins in late autumn and continues until early spring, except in periods of severe weather.*

shrub than as a tree (see page 110), and *Pittosporum* can form part of the background planting. They will grow in sun or part-shade; indeed the *Viburnum* and *Aucuba* will take full shade, and all will tolerate pruning. An ability to make new growth after pruning is a valuable asset for in order to obtain height you may have to choose shrubs which will in time become too wide for the space allocated. Obviously the largest kinds are best used in spacious gardens but even there some pruning may be needed from time to time to keep them dense.

While too much diversity in the background is not desirable, a solid planting of dark evergreens can be depressing, so it pays to add a few variegated evergreens or shrubs with lighter-colored foliage. *Elaeagnus* are particularly useful in this respect as during the growing season the shoots and young leaves of the variegated varieties are brownish or gray, reducing their impact; only in autumn and winter are the gold and green of *E. × ebbingei* 'Gilt Edge' and *E. pungens* 'Maculata' at their brightest. *Elaeagnus × ebbingei* is by far the most popular non-variegated member of this drought-tolerant family.

Its leaves are mid-green above and gray beneath and it makes a large specimen with the greatest rapidity, but it can also die without warning. More attractive, largely because both surfaces of its leaves are silvery, particularly in spring, is *E. macrophylla*. Although slow-growing, it eventually makes a large spreading shrub. Both these *Elaeagnus* produce small, sweetly scented flowers in autumn.

The rich yellow and green forms of *Euonymus japonicus* are less hardy than *Elaeagnus* and even more inclined to revert but they will certainly withstand heat and drought. The best variety for use as a background subject is *Euonymus japonicus* 'Duc d'Anjou' because its mixture of yellow, dark green and gray-green is pleasantly subdued.

In addition to a background of tall evergreen shrubs, the structure of the garden will be strengthened by a core of mainly shorter-growing evergreen shrubs. The majority should look neat and most should be able to withstand the worst extremes of the weather; positions where a failure would not be too catastrophic can be filled by the somewhat tender *Cistus* (see page 111) or *Escallonia* (see page 113).

The adjective "neat" is one I would certainly apply to hebes with their close-packed leaves and tidy compact forms. Their assets are considerable: their winter appearance is excellent; those that flower in midsummer will continue to produce blooms well into autumn; they tolerate strong winds provided these are not frost-laden; and do not mind light or heavy soil as long as it is well drained and the position sunny. Many make good ground cover. They strike easily from cuttings and recover well from pruning, yet rarely need it. Provided they are not required to cope with high temperatures or a dry atmosphere, they can survive drought, but on light soils it is advisable to ensure they have humus and a good mulch. Hebes vary considerably in their hardiness, however; those with small leaves generally are reasonably hardy.

Hebes originated in New Zealand, where they take the place of heather in the natural environment. Strangely, native British heather and ling and other ericas which are found elsewhere in Europe are not often recommended for dry gardens, perhaps because most of them grow in areas of high rainfall; yet they

Lathyrus latifolius
Although lacking the fragrance and large flower size of the sweet pea, the everlasting pea has undoubted qualities. It is perennial, although it dies down each winter, will grow in dry soils and is very adaptable. It can be set to climb a trellis or fence to a height of 6 ft., encouraged to ramble through a large shrub or rose, or planted to tumble down a bank. If the flowers are removed as they start to fade and old stems cut out to encourage new shoots, it will bloom all summer. The original form has magenta flowers but there are clear pink and lavender forms and the beautiful 'White Pearl' which comes from seed.

also inhabit some of the driest, poorest soils. Essentially wildings, they never look at home in a formal garden or when set among soft-leaved herbaceous plants. Not surprisingly, they associate best with shrubs that also enjoy sunny positions and thrive in well-drained soil, such as brooms, dwarf pines, *Helianthemum*, *Cistus*, hebes and junipers. In a small, intimate setting it may be possible to use odd single plants, but if they are to play a major part in forming the character of the garden, they need to be massed together, but not in a special bed with only conifers for company, as is so often seen, and preferably not in blocks of a single cultivar as this again imposes a quite unnatural formality.

Bell heather (*Erica cinerea*) and cross-leaved heath (*E. tetralix*) begin their long flowering season in midsummer and overlap with ling (*Calluna vulgaris*), which does not begin to show color until the beginning of autumn. They all need a lime-free soil. *Erica carnea* and *E. × darleyensis*, on the other hand, tolerate lime and are early-flowering species, beginning their display in the depths of winter and continuing to flower well into spring. Most other hardy heathers are intolerant of drought.

The soil preparation for heaths needs to be thorough. Dig in plenty of well-rotted compost, peat or pulverized bark, but not farmyard manure. Soak the plants thoroughly before they go in and be sure to apply a mulch. Young plants are particularly susceptible to drought so for the first year do not allow the soil to get dry.

Berberis look well with heathers, as they do with most other plants, and besides the tall ones there are many which are much shorter. *Berberis verruculosa*, for instance, is unlikely to grow much taller than 4 ft. Its spiny leaves, dark green above but silver beneath, are set on arching branches. In contrast, *B. gagnepainii* has narrow, ocean-green leaves and a neat, rounded habit. All have yellow flowers and will grow in either sun or shade, as will their relatives the mahonias. The Oregon grape (*Mahonia aquifolium*) is usually relegated to providing ground cover under trees but the newer, more compact cultivars 'Apollo' and 'Smaragd' deserve an open position, as long as

SHRUBS FOR
AUTUMN COLOR
Berberis × media
  'Park Jewel'
Berberis 'Rubrostilla'
Berberis thunbergii
  and cultivars
Berberis wilsoniae
Cotinus coggygria
  and cultivars
Cotinus obovatus
Cotoneaster divaricatus
Cotoneaster horizontalis
Euonymus alatus
Euonymus europaeus
Euonymus planipes
Rhus hirta
Ribes alpinum
Rosa rugosa
Rosa virginiana

This planting of several different forms of
Erica × darleyensis *in a setting of silver birch and large conifers exemplifies how heathers should be used where sufficient space is available.*

This cut-leaved form of the stag's horn sumach (Rhus hirta 'Laciniata') in its autumn dress is likely to be more brilliant than any other shrub or tree which can be grown in dry conditions. A large shrub of distinctive tree-like habit, it is very hardy, easily grown and useful for controlling erosion.

the soil is not dust dry, where their holly-like leaves will take on bronze tints in winter and they will freely produce deep golden flowers. The taller-growing *M. pinnata* withstands more drought.

Sarcococcas prefer shade and will not survive on a light soil if it is sunbaked. They are known as Christmas box because of their inconspicuous but powerfully scented winter flowers. There are several species; my own favorite is the 4 ft. tall *S. hookeriana digyna* which has glossy leaves that are more willow- than box-shaped and dark maroon stems. It slowly spreads by means of suckers. *Sarcococca confusa* grows only 2 ft. high and in time makes a weed-excluding thicket.

Cotoneaster dammeri is completely prostrate, its trailing shoots and comparatively large leaves forming a dense carpet. *Cotoneaster microphyllus* makes a low mound of tiny leaves, while *C. conspicuus* 'Decorus' is similar in appearance but grows about 3 ft. high, spreading to 8 ft. across. All of these have red berries and make excellent ground cover while their dark foliage offers useful contrast to silver or variegated plants.

Almost as dark as the cotoneasters, but with larger, glossier leaves, are two low-growing cousins of the cherry laurel, *Prunus laurocerasus* 'Otto Luyken' and 'Zabeliana.' Although eventually 3 ft. high by 6–10 ft. wide, they take many years to reach this size, especially on dry soils. The former has ascending branches, the latter horizontal, but on both the vertical racemes of small white flowers are carried rather like candles.

Few gray-leaved shrubs have sufficient good looks in winter for them to qualify as structural plants. The best known is *Brachyglottis* (syn. *Senecio*) 'Sunshine.' Jerusalem sage (*Phlomis fruticosa*) is a little less hardy but the yellow cast of its silvery leaves, together with its hooded, mustard-colored flowers, makes it excellent for associating with white *Cistus* or the young red leaves of *Photinia*. Another good companion is *Ceanothus thyrsiflorus repens*, probably the hardiest of several low, spreading forms of the Californian wild lilac due to its soft blue flowers and dark green leaves. *Ceanothus* 'Blue Mound' has smaller, even darker leaves and is more compact while its flowers are a richer blue.

Climbers and wall shrubs

Because the soil at the base of a wall will be dry even in a garden which receives adequate rainfall and has a naturally moisture-retentive soil, it might be assumed that the number of climbers for such a situation in the dry garden will be limited. As long as the soil preparation has been thorough, however, and water is given in the early stages, there are far more suitable plants than there will be positions to accommodate them even in a large garden.

The plants used to clothe a wall, fence or trellis are either true climbers like ivy, honeysuckle and climbing roses, or shrubs which are easy to train on flat surfaces such as *Chaenomeles* and *Cotoneaster*, or too tender to survive in the open. Just how big a risk you are prepared to take with climbers and shrubs which are native to hotter and drier countries than your own will depend on whether you can rig up some protection for them each winter and how much you mind if they are carried off by a particularly severe frost. My own philosophy is always to experiment, except where it really matters. If I had an ugly shed to hide, then I should want something dependable. Of course, the actual choice depends on where you live. In very cold areas some of the evergreen shrubs I have already mentioned like *Viburnum tinus* and even *Euphorbia characias* will need the protection of a wall or fence. If on the other hand your garden is not subject to a yearly dose of frost, you will be able to use the shrubs I shall recommend for warm walls out in the open garden and a new range of wall shrubs and climbers even more tender can take their place.

Sunny walls

Among evergreens for sunny walls ceanothus (see page 110) must take pride of place. I sometimes think it is worth gardening on dry sandy soil just for the sight of literally thousands of tiny blue flowers crowding their every branch. Even when out of flower their small, shiny, dark green leaves give pleasure and, additionally, they make an ideal background for later flowers. The best ceanothus need a lot of space as they easily can grow to a height

LOW-GROWING
SHRUBS FOR THE BASE
OF SUNNY WALLS
Abelia × grandiflora
Abelia schumannii
Artemisia arborescens
Callistemon salignus
*Ceratostigma
    willmottianum*
Cistus species
Coronilla glauca
Halimium species
Hebe hulkeana
Hebe speciosa
*Myrtus communis
    tarentina*
Nandina domestica
Phygelius capensis
Pittosporum tobira
Punica granatum nana
Rhaphiolepis species
Teucrium fruticans

of 13 ft. with a corresponding spread. The early-flowering *C. arboreus* 'Trewithen Blue' is one of the most spectacular with large pyramidal clusters of sky-blue flowers and comparatively large leaves. It has a reputation for being tender but seems no more so than many others. One of the hardiest is *C. thyrsiflorus* with light blue flowers, not to be confused with its low-spreading variety, *C. thyrsiflorus repens* (see page 111), although this can be useful against a low wall or under a window.

Another evergreen of rapid growth is *Escallonia* 'Iveyi.' Its leaves, large for an *Escallonia*, are glossy and dark green, making a perfect foil for the large panicles of pure white flowers in late summer. Even more beautiful but less hardy still is *E. bifida*, also with white flowers but in early autumn. Both can grow to 13 ft. tall. Other *Escallonia* benefit from being trained on or grown in front of a wall; except in very cold areas they can be in partial shade.

If you are interested in making a show, then plant *Fremontodendron* 'California Glory.' In early summer it will be covered with large, single, cup-shaped flowers in a brilliant shade of golden yellow. After a rest it will continue to flower less spectacularly into the autumn. The fig-shaped leaves are brownish-green. Tall-growing and needing a house wall to do it full justice, it is said to need a sandy soil but I have found some of the best examples on well-drained clay. *Fremontodendron* has two disadvantages: the dead flowers remain on the twigs fading to orange and brown, while the rust-colored hairs which coat the backs of the leaves and young shoots can irritate nose and eyes, making pruning an unpleasant task.

Abutilon vitifolium shares some of the characteristics of *Fremontodendron*. It, too, makes rapid upright growth and its leaves and shoots are downy but in their case grayish and causing no problems. The delightful sky-blue, pale mauve or white, cup-

ABOVE **Clematis armandii** *displays its almond-scented flowers at the top of a wall in Italy. In such a hot climate it will need watering every week in summer. In cooler lands it can tolerate quite a dry position but needs a sheltered, sunny wall.*

FAR LEFT *Aspect is the first constraint to be considered when selecting a climber. Here, ivy thrives on the shady sides of the walls while grape vines make their home on those in the sun.*

71

Among the very few blue-flowered shrubs which grow to a large size, the evergreen Ceanothus — here C. impressus — are outstanding. In all but the most favored gardens they will need the protection of a warm wall.

shaped flowers are produced in clusters in early summer. *Abutilon megapotamicum* is completely different. Its thin and lax stems make it easy to train, its narrow leaves are dark green, and its flowers, which hang like Christmas decorations along every twig, resemble those of a fuchsia but with a scarlet calyx and yellow petals. The flowers of the hybrid *A.* 'Kentish Belle' are larger, the calyces dusky red and the skirt-like petals pale gold with faint red veins.

Some evergreens when planted against a wall become like living buttresses, which require only the minimum of pruning. *Pittosporum tenuifolium* is a good example, particularly in the case of its variegated or colored leaf forms which are less hardy. Another is the common myrtle *(Myrtus communis)* whose leaves emit a spicy scent when crushed, as do its small white flowers whose numerous yellow stamens give the flowers a fluffy appearance.

Some tender buddleias are good for sunny walls. *Buddleia crispa* is, perhaps, the most attractive because its leaves and stems and even its buds have a pale green, velvety covering. The pale pinky-lilac flowers are produced over a lengthy period in later summer. The long, dark green leaves of *B. colvilei* tend to hang vertically, giving it a somewhat dejected look, but its drooping panicles of large, deep pink flowers are sumptuous and quite unlike those of the normal butterfly bush *(B. davidii)*.

Buddleia auriculata is grown for the delicious scent given off from short creamy spikes in early winter.

Many popular climbers do well in dry soils once they are established. Wisteria, *Vitis vinifera* 'Purpurea' and *V. coignetiae*, jasmines and *Passiflora caerulea* will all withstand drought in cool climates but may need an occasional thorough soaking in hotter ones. Climbing roses, on the whole, seem to do better on dry soil than equivalent shrubby sorts but you need to choose those described as vigorous, water them well when young and do not give up if they appear miserable for the first year or two. I have the old, sweetly scented *Rosa* 'Madame Alfred Carrière' on a partially shaded wall; its roots are in a raised bed and the soil is often like dust, yet it is never watered. Although it suffers from mildew, it produces quantities of large pinky white flowers and every autumn it has to be hard pruned to keep it below the eaves of the house.

Opinions on the suitability of honeysuckles for the dry garden vary. *Lonicera japonica* will certainly take drought as will *L. etrusca* and *L. splendida*, although these also need heat. Those originating from cooler climes are best with their roots in the shade although they do like to get their heads into the sun, as happens in their natural woodland homes.

Everyone agrees that clematis need plenty of moisture but the winter- and spring-flowering spe-

TALL SHRUBS FOR
SUNNY WALLS
Acacia dealbata
Acacia retinodes
Aloysia triphylla
Buddleja fallowiana alba
Callistemon salignus
Carpenteria californica
Cytisus battandieri
Grevillea rosmarinifolia
Magnolia grandiflora
Piptanthus laburnifolius
Rhamnus alaternus
variegatus
Robinia hispida 'Rosea'

The covering for a shady wall need not lack color. Here, the tiny leaves and bright red berries of Cotoneaster microphyllus are displayed against the large leaves of variegated Persian ivy (Hedera colchica 'Dentata Variegata'), showing that it can pay to let climbers mingle. Steps may have to be taken to ensure that the ivy does not eventually engulf the cotoneaster.

cies like *C. armandii*, with its long, leathery evergreen leaves and clusters of white flowers, *C. alpina* and *C. macropetala*, with small, nodding blue flowers, and the incredibly vigorous *C. montana* all tolerate quite dry conditions. If you are determined to have a clematis that flowers later in the year, concentrate on the small-flowered *C. texensis*, *C. tangutica* and *C. viticella* or some of their cultivars.

Among more exotic climbers are those which need the heat of a sunny wall if they are to flower freely. *Campsis × tagliabuana* 'Madame Galen' bears salmon-red trumpet flowers in late summer. Although it is supposed to be self-clinging, it is best to give it some support, otherwise the heavy stems will cause it to fall away from the wall. For a red brick wall the butter-yellow *C. radicans flava* can be a better choice. The purple-blue flowers of *Solanum crispum* 'Glasnevin' show its relationship to the potato; it is fast-growing and has a long season but is a laggard by comparison with *S. jasminoides* 'Album' which is about the quickest-growing and longest-flowering plant I know. A young plant put out as soon as the danger of frost has passed will make a good display in its first season. Regrettably, it is none too hardy. The star-shaped white flowers with a yellow center have no scent, in spite of the name. The small, jasmine-like flowers of *Trachelospermum jasminoides* are fragrant, however, and its neat evergreen leaves glossy.

Shady walls

If the soil on the shady side of a wall or fence is protected from the main moisture-bearing winds, it may be every bit as dry as that which receives the sun. There are several shrubs for shady walls which can be either trained along horizontal wires or allowed to grow more naturally, simply being clipped back when they grow out too far.

Cotoneaster, *Pyracantha* and *Garrya elliptica*, which bears long green catkins in mid-winter, are examples of suitable evergreens; Japanese quince or japonica (*Chaenomeles*) and *Forsythia suspensa* are among useful deciduous shrubs.

Climbers which can hoist themselves heavenward without special help, other than the provision of a wall or fence, are few but some of the best that do will grow in dry shade. The leaves of the true Virginia creeper (*Parthenocissus quinquefolia*) are usually composed of five leaflets. Boston ivy *(P. tricuspidata)* has maple-shaped leaves and, confusingly, is also sometimes known as Virginia creeper. *Parthenocissus henryana* is particularly attractive as its veins are picked out in silver and pink. All are rampant and color up like woodfires in autumn. Ivy, by comparison, sounds dull but there is a wide range of leaf shape and size to choose from while the variegated sorts provide year-round color.

SHRUBS AND CLIMBERS
FOR SHADY WALLS
Celastrus scandens
Chaenomeles species
Cotoneaster franchetii
Cotoneaster horizontalis
Cotoneaster lacteus
Euonymus fortunei
Fallopia baldschuanica
× *Fatshedera lizei*
Garrya elliptica
Hedera species
Jasminum nudiflorum
Kerria japonica
Lonicera species
Parthenocissus species
Pyracantha species

A shady border

Most shade-loving plants need a moist rooting medium so dry soil in shade presents a particular challenge. The wall in this garden, shown in early spring, casts a shadow on the border plants, but also provides some protection from drying winds and hot sunshine. As a result, the choice of plants that can be grown is much wider.

Very narrow borders against walls should be avoided where possible. Here, the border measures between 3 ft. and 8 ft., allowing room for foreground shrubs and plants as well as climbers and wall shrubs. Spring bulbs would bring additional seasonal color. Purple crocuses would look delightful with the lime-green flowers of the hellebores; snowdrops or white *Scilla siberica* 'Alba' could be grouped among the purple leaves of the viola, and massed grape hyacinths would complement the new, yellowish foliage of the euonymus.

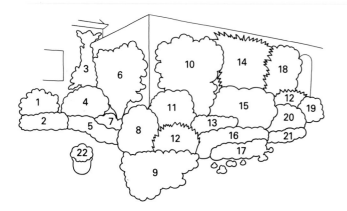

1 *Chaenomeles × superba* 'Rowallane': deciduous shrub with rich orange-red flowers in early spring and golden edible quinces in autumn; horizontal in habit, it is unlikely to grow much above 5 ft.

2 *Arum italicum italicum*: the new autumn leaves of this summer-dormant tuberous perennial are arrow-shaped, with every vein picked out in palest green, and by spring they are 2 ft. tall; after they have died away in late summer spikes of red berries appear; needs shade and plenty of humus.

3 *Hedera helix* 'Glacier': self-clinging ivy, climbing to 10 ft., with small gray-green leaves edged and splashed with white.

4 *Choisya ternata* 'Sundance' (Mexican orange blossom): yellow-leaved cultivar of the evergreen shrub, growing slowly to 6 ft., with fragrant white flowers in late spring.

5 *Euphorbia amygdaloides robbiae*: evergreen perennial with greenish-yellow, bracted flowers on 2½ ft. tall stems, produced in spring from rosettes of dark green leaves.

6 *Cotoneaster lacteus*: fast-growing evergreen shrub with leathery leaves, dark green above and gray beneath, and clusters of red berries from late autumn to spring; trained on a wall it can reach 13 ft.

7 *Digitalis grandiflora*: evergreen perennial foxglove; narrow basal leaves; 2½ ft. high spikes of sulfur-yellow flowers, netted chocolate-brown within, in early summer.

8 *Lonicera nitida* 'Baggesen's Gold': evergreen foliage shrub, 4 ft. tall, with tiny rounded leaves, golden in summer, turning yellowish-green in autumn.

14 *Jasminum nudiflorum* (winter jasmine): a most dependable winter-flowering climber, excellent for a sunless wall and capable of growing to 13 ft.; yellow flowers on leafless green stems open in mild spells from autumn until spring.

15 *Aucuba japonica* 'Rozannie': evergreen shrub, growing slowly to 6 ft., with large dark leaves and scarlet berries in winter.

16 *Helleborus argutifolius* (syn. *H. corsicus*): evergreen perennial making a bushy plant 2 ft. tall with divided holly-like leaves and clusters of pale green, cup-shaped flowers for many weeks in late winter and spring.

17 *Viola labradorica*: violet with small purplish-green leaves and masses of tiny purple but unscented flowers on 1 in. long stems from late winter to early spring.

18 *Garrya elliptica*: long jade-green catkins shaded with pink decorate this 10 ft. tall evergreen shrub in winter or early spring; best grown against a sunny wall in very cold areas.

19 *Euonymus fortunei* 'Emerald Gaiety': evergreen foliage shrub of fairly open habit, growing 3 ft. high but much wider; white-edged leaves tinged pink in winter.

20 *Brunnera macrophylla*: herbaceous perennial, sometimes called giant forget-me-not, with 1½ ft. tall sprays of blue spring flowers held above small, heart-shaped leaves; these grow to make good ground cover; plenty of humus is needed on light soils.

21 *Geranium macrorrhizum* 'Album': hardy, semi-evergreen perennial with light green, fragrant leaves, the oldest turning red or orange in autumn; white flowers are produced in early summer on 1 ft. stems.

22 *Rhododendron yakushimanum*: dwarf species ideal for a container filled with ericaceous compost; pink buds open to white flowers in late spring to early summer, while the young, silvery leaves gradually mature to dark green with brown felted undersides.

9 *Bergenia* 'Sunningdale': evergreen perennial with large glossy leaves, maroon above and red beneath in winter, and deep pink flowers on 1½ ft. reddish stems in spring.

10 *Rhamnus alaternus* 'Argenteovariegatus': fast-growing, evergreen shrub with small, marbled leaves, edged with white; inconspicuous flowers and small, red, autumn berries; in cold areas it needs the shelter of a wall on which it will reach at least 10 ft.

11 *Mahonia pinnata*: 5 ft. tall, sturdy evergreen shrub, with ocean-green prickly leaves and yellow flowers in early spring.

12 *Iris foetidissima citrina*: clumps of shiny green leaves, 2 ft. long, provide year-round interest; soft yellow flowers give rise to fat green pods in autumn; these turn brown and split to reveal rows of brilliant red berries.

13 *Dryopteris filix-mas*: the male fern will thrive in dry and poor soils if given shelter from wind; each spring it sends up "shuttlecocks" of 3 ft., mid-green fronds from brown scaly rhizomes; it will remain attractive until cut down by hard frosts.

Plants for the foreground

Plants for the front edge of a border need choosing and arranging with particular care. Always visible, they should have attractive foliage like that of *Dianthus*, *Epimedium* or *Hebe*. Avoid anything which requires staking or which goes through an untidy stage, as do most bearded iris after they have flowered. If the border is viewed from a principal window or is situated near an entrance, then the plant's winter appearance needs to be considered. *Bergenia*, *Libertia* and *Helleborus argutifolius* (syn. *H. corsicus*) would be worth having for their winter foliage even if they never flowered. At the same time, the foreground planting should not distract the eye from the main area of interest which will normally lie further back in the border.

Too much variety with one of this and one of that also produces a restless feeling. A better method is to plant quite long drifts of the same plant set closely enough to make a solid block, rather than allowing them to be seen as a group of individuals. Nearly all low shrubs and hardy plants described as "ground cover" produce this effect. Between the drifts plant smaller groups of plants of contrasting habit, or even single individuals if they are sufficiently bold. This is a position where an ornamental grass with clumps of narrow arching leaves and tall seed heads can be useful. A single plant of *Stipa gigantea* with its fan of 6 ft. tall stems carrying golden oat-like heads may be sufficient in a shrub border, while *Pennisetum alopecuroides* which has indigo bottlebrush flowers at half the height or *Helictotrichon sempervirens* with silvery blue blades may be sufficient among low-growing herbaceous plants.

Potentillas, which are able to withstand moderate drought on any sort of soil as long as the climate is a cool one, are often used as a foreground shrub. They have an extremely long flowering season, pleasing small leaves which can be green or gray depending on the cultivar and rounded habit, but their tendency to retain some of their withered leaves in winter, particularly in sheltered gardens, gives them a bedraggled look especially in wet weather. They are as a result best used in less prominent positions.

Foliage interest

Just as the restrained use of a few tall shrubs with variegated or gray leaves will improve a background, so the inclusion of some dwarf shrubs or hardy plants with variegated or silvery leaves at the front of borders will point up the more usual greens. If their colors are sufficiently bright, they will help to compensate for the absence of flowers during winter. Some of the cultivars of *Euonymus fortunei*, such as 'Silver Queen,' 'Emerald Gaiety,' 'Emerald 'n' Gold' and 'Canadale Gold,' fulfill this purpose admirably. All these *Euonymus* make a dense, ground-covering mound about 1½ ft. tall and 3 ft. across but growth is not quick and unless your garden is small it is better to plant in groups allowing no more than 2 ft. between individuals.

There are several variegated forms of box, including *Buxus sempervirens* 'Elegantissima,' with narrow, dark green leaves edged with yellow, and *B. sempervirens* 'Latifolia Maculata' whose young leaves are almost entirely gold. Like ordinary green box these can be clipped into geometric shapes such as pyramids, cubes or balls and used singly as a focal point or repeated along the front of a border at regular intervals to punctuate looser planting.

Few variegated herbaceous plants are suitable for dry soils but these are among the best. *Iris pallida* has glaucous leaves striped with white in the form 'Argenteo' and yellow in 'Aurea Variegata.' Rather small lavender flowers are produced but it is for the summer-long display of their handsome leaves that they are grown. I like 'Argenteo' in association with the plum-gray foliage and wine-red flowers of *Sedum* 'Ruby Glow,' and the yellow-and-gray sword-shaped leaves of 'Aurea Variegata' as contrast for a drift of the dark, wiry little bushes of *Calamintha nepeta* with their clouds of pale blue flowers from late summer. *Sisyrinchium striatum* 'Aunt May' also has iris-shaped leaves with creamy yellow stripes on a gray-green background but they are much smaller. The straw-colored flowers are arranged vertically on stems which stand above the leaves. It makes an excellent foreground plant for *rugosa* roses.

ABOVE *These double borders have been planted with a continuous band of Nepeta 'Six Hills Giant.' The use of a single plant on this scale allows the eye to concentrate on the vista and discourages the walker from loitering.*

RIGHT *Intricately planted mixed borders of this type need to be examined in detail and the foreground planting should not hurry one along. At the same time a certain amount of repetition, here achieved with yellow-green Alchemilla mollis, strengthens the design.*

LOW GROUND COVER
FOR SUN

*Anthemis punctata
    cupaniana*
Arctostaphylos uva-ursi
Armeria maritima
Artemisia 'Powis Castle'
Ballota pseudodictamnus
Calluna vulgaris
    and cultivars
Centaurea hypoleuca
    'John Coutts'
Cerastium tomentosum
Chamaemelum nobile
Cistus × corbariensis
    (syn. *C. × hybridus*)
Cistus × skanbergii
Erica cinerea
    and cultivars
Erigeron glaucus
Eriophyllum lanatum
Euphorbia polychroma
Genista hispanica
Genista pilosa
Halimium lasianthum
Hebe pinguifolia 'Pagei'
Hebe rakaiensis
Hyssopus officinalis
Juniperus—
    prostrate forms
Leptinella squalida
Lotus hirsutus
Ophiopogon japonicus
Origanum vulgare
Osteospermum jucundum
Othonna cheirifolia
Phlox subulata
Rosa nitida
Salvia officinalis
Santolina species
Sedum spurium
Thymus species

Fronting a lawn

Where a shrub border is fronted by a lawn, it is better to use shrubs of neat rounded or upright habit in the front row such as rue (*Ruta*), *Genista hispanica*, *Santolina* and the shorter kinds of *Cistus* like *C. crispus* 'Sunset' and 'Silver Pink.' The distance you allow between the edge of the bed and the stem of the plant is critical. If you do not provide sufficient room for development, you may have to prune the shrub too hard in order to stop it from spoiling the grass; too much and you will be left with a gap of bare soil even after several years' growth. Herbaceous plants are much easier to control as, with few exceptions, they can be replanted further from the edge during the next planting season if a mistake has been made.

Plants for paving and gravel

Unlike grass, paving and gravel do not suffer if plants spill on to them; indeed, it is often desirable to mask the junction between soil and gravel or soften the hard edges of paving. Low, mat-forming rock plants like *Cerastium*, *Sedum spurium* and dwarf thymes are ideal as an edging to a narrow path, but where the path is wider there may be room for perennial candytuft (*Iberis sempervirens*), *Achillea tomentosa*, *Nepeta* or *Helianthemum*, all of which can make cushions 2 ft. across. Should the path be in shade, its edges can be softened by the trailing shoots of periwinkle (*Vinca*), the rosettes of London pride (*Saxifraga umbrosa*) or the dark mats made by the strawberry-like leaves of *Waldsteinia ternata* which in spring are lit by sprays of yellow flowers. If the paving is extensive, as with a terrace, something taller may be more appropriate. This is the perfect place for rosemary (*Rosmarinus*), allowing room for it to sprawl and thus avoiding the pruning which so often spoils its appearance, especially in old age. Lavender (*Lavandula*), *Santolina*, *Cistus*, *Convolvulus cneorum* and *Salvia officinalis* are other sun lovers that always look well when planted against paving.

Softening the edges of paving with plants is often desirable, but if the edging is attractively detailed, as in this skillful use of granite cobblestones, discretion is necessary. Included here, edging the border, are Helichrysum italicum with narrow, gray leaves and yellow flowers, Santolina rosmarinifolia rosmarinifolia with feathery foliage and button flowers still in bud, and pink-flowered Diascia. In the center, a yucca with its spiky rosette stands over a white-flowered Salvia argentea.

LOW GROUND COVER
FOR SHADE

Bergenia cordifolia
Brunnera macrophylla
Cotoneaster dammeri
Cotoneaster horizontalis
Cotoneaster microphyllus
Epimedium
 perralderianum
Euphorbia amygdaloides
 robbiae
Geranium endressii
Geranium
 'Johnson's Blue'
Geranium macrorrhizum
Geranium × *oxonianum*
 'Claridge Druce'
Geranium phaeum
Geranium sanguineum
Geranium wallichianum
 'Buxton's Variety'
Hedera algeriensis
 and cultivars
Hedera colchica
 and cultivars
Hedera helix and cultivars
Hypericum calycinum
Hypericum × *moserianum*
Lamium maculatum
Lonicera pileata
Pachysandra terminalis
Pulmonaria species
Pyracantha coccinea
 'Red Cushion'
Rubus pentalobus
Rubus tricolor
Sarcococca hookeriana
 humilis
Sarcococca ruscifolia
Symphoricarpos ×
 chenaultii 'Hancock'
Vinca minor
Waldsteinia ternata

The junction between gravel and soil is always best hidden. Here the edging plants include pinks (Dianthus), rock roses (Helianthemum), mauve catmint (Nepeta), and Sedum. Clumps of iris provide spiky contrast.

Plants for retaining walls

Nearly all the prostrate, wide-spreading plants which soften the outlines of paving will, if planted near the top of a retaining wall, cascade down its face. There are many others—which you choose will depend on the height of the wall and the amount of it you wish to decorate with plants. Ivy, summer and winter jasmine and some other climbers will hang down as well as grow up. Prostrate junipers like *Juniperus conferta* and *J. communis* 'Hornibrookii' will trail by as much as 8 ft.; *Cotoneaster horizontalis* and *Euonymus radicans vegetus* are more restrained. *Euphorbia myrsinites*, *Aubrieta*, *Alyssum* and *Phlox subulata* never look better than when tumbling over a low wall. For a late-summer display they need to be interplanted with *Gypsophila* 'Rosenschleier,' which makes a pale pink cloud as much as 3 ft. across, and *Convolvulus sabatius* with lavender-blue funnels on trailing shoots, a rather tender plant which is likely to live longer if it can get its roots well down behind a wall.

Edging plants

It may be that instead of blurring a line you will wish to emphasize it, translating it from the horizontal into the vertical. Such is the purpose of a dwarf hedge traditionally made from edging box (*Buxus sempervirens* 'Suffruticosa'), or in hotter countries from *B. microphylla koreana*, and used to outline a flower bed or create the patterns in a parterre or knot garden. Beds can also be edged with *Santolina*, rue or *Teucrium chamaedrys*, a soft-wooded sub-shrub often used as an edging to herb gardens, but they will need clipping several times each summer. Lavenders, like the sumptuously colored *Lavandula angustifolia* 'Hidcote,' are often used around beds of roses, and where the soil is dry enough for lavenders to do well but sufficiently rich and moist for roses, the combination is one of the best sights and scents in the garden. However, as a hedge, lavenders have their limitations. Their long flower stalks produce a rounded outline while their winter appearance can be grim.

Plants for focus

In every garden there are positions where a plant with a bold shape, sculptured leaves or bizarre form is needed. It may be required as a major focal point as at the end of a vista, or to mark a change in direction or level. Most often its purpose is to add drama to an area of planting, or relieve the monotony which can result when too many plants of the same height or texture are assembled. If these feature plants which are frequently described as "architectural" or "sculptured" are to make their full impact, they need to stand clear of other plants of the same height, preferably rising from low ground cover, and they must not be overdone; one or two planted singly or in small groups in a given area will be sufficient unless you consciously decide to let them dominate a part of the garden, dictating its style as, for instance, an assembly of yuccas might do.

Columnar plants

When looking for living spires and columns, conifers first come to mind with the Italian cypress (*Cupressus sempervirens*) setting the standard. Although usually considered somewhat tender, it can be grown in the U.S. and Britain—I have two in my own garden which are now 13 ft. tall; they were propagated from seed taken from a tree which has been growing in a local churchyard for over sixty years and which was itself the offspring of a tree in the Garden of Gethsemane. They are said to be much more tender when young and once over head height are less likely to be damaged by frost and, doubtless, they are more likely to survive on a dry soil. Failing a cypress, there are several suitable columnar junipers, although none will grow quite so tall. *Juniperus virginiana* 'Skyrocket' is the best known, while Irish yew (*Taxus baccata* 'Fastigiata') and its golden counterpart 'Fastigiata Aurea' make robust, stubby columns.

Weeping plants

For a pendulous effect, we must look to deciduous trees. There are weeping forms of *Robinia*, *Gleditsia* and *Sophora* but they are rare and can be rather difficult to obtain. There will be no such problem, however, with the weeping silver pear (*Pyrus salicifo-*

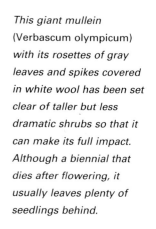

This giant mullein (Verbascum olympicum) with its rosettes of gray leaves and spikes covered in white wool has been set clear of taller but less dramatic shrubs so that it can make its full impact. Although a biennial that dies after flowering, it usually leaves plenty of seedlings behind.

lia 'Pendula') but it may need some pampering and, as it transplants badly, you are well advised to seek out a well-grown plant in a container.

If you are prepared to go to the trouble, *Buddleia alternifolia* can be trained into a small weeping tree by reducing the young plant to a single shoot and tying this to a stake. When it has reached the top of the stake, the head can be allowed to develop with the branches gracefully arching outward, to be wreathed in midsummer with honey-scented lilac flowers. The Mount Etna broom (*Genista aetnensis*) also has thin, semi-pendulous branches which resemble a golden fountain during the summer months, but its tree-like habit can be encouraged and emphasized by supporting the main stem in the early stages of growth with a stout cane.

Horizontal plants

Plants of horizontal growth make a striking composition when combined with a narrow, upright tree and even on their own can create a strong accent. *Juniperus × media* 'Pfitzeriana' and 'Pfitzeriana Aurea' have feathery, semi-horizontal branches which produce a multi-layered effect, but by the time they are 3 ft. tall they will be 8 ft. wide and still growing, so they are not for confined spaces. *Juniperus × media* 'Gold Coast' is more compact. Altogether smaller but still producing an excellent horizontal line is the gray-green *J. sabina* 'Tamariscifolia.' *Cotoneaster horizontalis* is most often seen spread against a wall but it did not receive its name without reason and its fan-like growths will cover 6 ft. while only rising 2 ft. high.

The flowerheads of Sedum *and the golden* Helenium *create a "platform" which makes them the perfect contrast for the vertical torches of* Kniphofia. *However, a basically spiky plant such as the purple* Salvia × superba *will, if massed as here, also produce a horizontal line. The* Helenium *needs reasonable moisture but the scarlet* Epilobium *enjoys heat and drought.*

81

Bold foliage

A plant which has leaves much larger than one would expect from its overall size is bound to be arresting, and even though plants which have adapted to dry soils frequently have small leaves, there are, nonetheless, exceptions. These are particularly dramatic when used in the dry garden. *Catalpa speciosa* has heart-shaped leaves 1 ft. long which give it a tropical appearance, although it will survive low temperatures as well as heat. Its foxglove-like flowers are white spotted with purple and followed by long seed pods. Reaching 60 ft. high and 50 ft. wide, it makes a slightly bigger tree than the much better known Indian bean tree *(C. bignonioides)*, which requires more moisture.

The Japanese angelica tree *(Aralia elata)* is a suckering shrub about 12 ft. tall. The huge, double pinnate leaves cluster at the top of the stems and in late summer are surmounted by plumes of white flowers. When bereft of its leaves, its gaunt, spiny stems are objects of curiosity rather than beauty. Stag's horn sumach *(Rhus hirta*, syn. *R. typhina)* is another tall-growing shrub with pinnate leaves, which all occur at the tops of the stems, producing a flat-topped appearance. You must be prepared to remove its suckers or allow them to develop into a thicket. The leaves color brilliantly in autumn, then fall to reveal the tawny velvet which covers the young branches.

The leaves of *Mahonia japonica* and the more elegant but frost-tender *M. lomariifolia* are basically the same shape as those of the *Rhus* but are evergreen, leathery, have spines and are held at an angle to the stem. This gives the plants a sculptured appearance.

The leaves of *Fatsia japonica* are even more impressive. They are like big green hands with seven wavy-edged fingers held out horizontally on long stalks. The shrub grows 8 ft. tall and wide, and carries clusters of white flowers in round heads in autumn. Mexican orange blossom *(Choisya ternata)* is excellent where a dense, rounded but less exotic evergreen is required. Its dark green mature leaves, highly polished and formed of three leaflets, throw into relief the lighter green young leaves. Clusters of white, sweetly-fragrant, star-shaped flowers are produced freely in spring, with a sprinkling in late

summer. Like *Fatsia*, it needs shelter from icy winds and will take shade except in colder areas where both plants need the protection of a wall.

Although classed as a shrub, *Melianthus* behaves more like a herbaceous plant in cool climates. My own plant escaped the frost once and, as a result, managed to produce in spring rather second-rate maroon flowers on a 6 ft. stem which hardly seemed to compensate for the fact that the foliage by then looked decidedly tatty. Normally, the small pale green shoots push through the bracken fern mulch with which I have protected the plant rather late in the spring and then grow steadily to a height of about 3 ft. or so and a spread of 5 ft. The spectacular leaves are 1 ft. long, pinnate and divided into sharply toothed leaflets. By autumn the color has deepened to a blue-gray.

ABOVE *The huge leaves of the cardoon* (Cynara cardunculus), *planted here with purple* Salvia haematodes, *provide a dramatic ingredient for the summer garden.*

ABOVE RIGHT *Although occurring naturally in damp meadowlands,* Miscanthus sinensis *is remarkably adaptable. Different cultivars are available, which vary in their freedom of flowering and autumn coloring.*

be in the vicinity of water and doubtless they prefer plenty of moisture when they can get it, but they are less likely to be killed by frosts if their crowns are dry in winter. Even so, those with stripy colored leaves should be protected.

The leaves of phormiums all spring from ground level and are arranged rather like a fan, whereas those of yuccas (see page 117) are arranged in rosettes and lean outward, giving them a markedly more spiky appearance and sculptural quality. There is probably no other hardy plant whose appearance is so evocative of heat and drought, although *Cistus* is more redolent of sunbaked hillsides.

There are several perennials whose bold foliage or distinctive form equip them for prominent positions. *Acanthus* and *Euphorbia* are described in the chapter "Key plants" (see pages 118 and 120). Bergenias evoke strong responses; garden designers in cool countries love them for their big, rounded, evergreen leaves, invaluable for providing solidity and contrast to feathery textures and for their ground-covering abilities. Their clients are often less enthusiastic! This may be due to the vivid magenta coloring of the flowers of *B. cordifolia* which, with its form 'Purpurea,' are the best for poor dry soils. If you are one of those whose dislike is for the color, try *B.* 'Bressingham White' or 'Bressingham Salmon' but you will need to incorporate plenty of compost or manure if your soil is a poor one.

Ornamental grasses

Grasses, whose leaves and not just their flower stems are tall, can be almost as impressive as spiky or large-leaved plants, but in a much lighter and airy way. The various elegant forms of *Miscanthus sinensis* will grow quite well on dry soils, although they do much better on moist, well-drained ones, but pampas grass (*Cortaderia selloana*) can survive heat, cold and drought. Unfortunately, all too often it is seen lording it over some cramped urban front garden. However, given a park-like setting of trees and shrubs, where its silvery plumes can be set against some autumn-coloring trees, it takes on an entirely different character. In a medium-sized garden it is best to let it dominate an area by planting a group in a border of low junipers, rue or *Berberis wilsoniae*.

ORNAMENTAL GRASSES
Briza media
Deschampsia caespitosa
Elymus magellanicus
Festuca amethystina
Festuca glauca
Festuca punctoria
Helictotrichon
  sempervirens
Holcus mollis
  'Albovariegatus'
Hordeum jubatum
Millium effusum 'Aureum'
Pennisetum alopecuroides
Pennisetum orientale
Stipa arundinacea
Stipa calamagrostis

Leaves do not have to be excessively large to be eye-catching; it is sufficient for them to depart from the run-of-the-mill shape as do those which are sword- or strap-shaped. Even the 2 ft. tall foliage of bearded iris, daylilies (*Hemerocallis*) and blue or white *Agapanthus* will always stand out in a herbaceous border. The most dramatic sword leaves belong to New Zealand flax (*Phormium tenax*); they are held erect and grow to a height of 8 ft., even on dry soils. In the species they are dusty green but soft purple-brown in 'Purpureum,' and dramatically edged with yellow in 'Variegatum.' The summer flowers are like dull red brackets at the top of tall stems. *Phormium cookianum* is shorter and has arching leaves. There are numerous cultivars, some no taller than 1 ft., my own favorites being 'Cream Delight' and 'Sundowner.' The most luxuriant always seem to

Color in the garden

When it comes to choosing permanent plants which are grown principally for their flowers, we all have our favorites, but we should not overlook the need for continuity of interest throughout the garden and in every season. Equally, the role that is played by colored foliage plants in providing garden color at potentially dull times of the year should not be underestimated.

Gardens can be colorful without flowers as this picture shows. Yellow is provided by Berberis thunbergii *'Aurea' and in the foreground by* Euonymus fortunei *'Emerald n' Gold.' The blue filigree foliage belongs to* Ruta graveolens *'Jackman's Blue' and the olive-green is that of* Hebe cupressoides. *Gray lavender and purple* Prunus × cistena *make smaller contributions.*

Foliage plants

The addition of even a small amount of colored foliage will make a contribution entirely out of proportion to the amount of space it occupies, so it should be positioned with care; in particular it needs to relate to the planting around it. Flower gardens based on a single color are popular but much of their effect depends on the foliage plants with which the flowers are combined. White flowers seem whiter when interplanted with gray foliage, the golden garden needs a background of yellow-leaved shrubs while a red border would be unthinkable without purple-leaved *Berberis* and *Cotinus*. It is only a step from this to consider devoting part of the garden to shrubs and foliage plants of a restricted color range where flowers play a subsidiary role.

Silver foliage

It is difficult to think of any part of the garden where the addition of some silver or blue-gray foliage will not prove beneficial. It adds light where green or purple foliage looks too dark, tones down blatant colors or provides a perfect setting for flowers of pastel shades. The great silvery cardoon (*Cynara cardunculus*) can be used as a summer focal point, as can the tall barbaric Scotch thistle (*Onopordum acanthium*) and *Verbascum olympicum* which makes a rosette of felt-covered leaves 3 ft. across and in its second year sends up thin silvery spires dotted with yellow flowers. Some silvery plants look positively metallic and can dominate any group of plants; *Senecio cineraria* 'White Diamond' and *Eryngium giganteum* are examples. Rue (*Ruta*), sea kale (*Crambe maritima*) and other plants of glaucous hue are soft and shadowy

RIGHT *In this classic combination of white flowers and silvery foliage, silver is provided by the teasle-like heads of* Eryngium giganteum, *finely cut* Senecio cineraria, *Scotch thistle* (Onopordum acanthium) *and the thin spikes of* Artemisia ludoviciana. *The white flowers are love-in-a-mist* (Nigella), *the curving spikes of* Lysimachia clethroides, *the Shasta daisy* (Chrysanthemum × superbum) *and the tall spires of* Veronicastrum virginicum album.

Lychnis coronaria

The rose campion arrived in England from its home in southern Europe during the fourteenth century. Its basal rosettes of leaves and its 3 ft. tall branching stems are coated in fine silvery hairs which help conserve moisture. The flat circular flowers are a striking shade of crimson-magenta, or white in L. coronaria Alba Group and white with a pink center in the Oculata Group—a relief from the yellow flowers so often produced by gray-leaved plants. The strident magenta shade can be tempered by a setting of pink or pale blue flowers, but the adventurous may risk raised eyebrows by combining it with apricot or purple. Although short-lived, self-sown seedlings are freely produced and transplant easily.

and when planted at the far end of a border they can make it appear longer. By using *Lamium maculatum* 'Beacon Silver' and 'White Nancy,' we can even have silver foliage in the shade.

The owners of a dry, sunny and reasonably warm garden are presented with the ideal conditions for an all-gray garden, using perhaps a few purple shrubs for contrast and accent. When it comes to making a selection, they are spoiled for choice. There are the feathery artemisias which can be contrasted with the plain felted leaves of *Stachys byzantina* 'Silver Carpet,' fine-textured *Hebe pimeleoides* 'Quicksilver' and woolly-leaved *Salvia argentea*, dwarf shrubs like *Santolina* and *Helichrysum splendidum* and grasses such as the steely *Helictotrichon sempervirens* and powder-blue *Festuca glauca* best used in sizable drifts. Backgrounds can be composed of *Atriplex halimus*, *Romneya coulteri*, *Cytisus battandieri* and *Buddleia fallowiana alba*, and, if the scale is large enough, *Eucalyptus gunnii*. The eucalyptus will need to be cut almost to the ground each spring to keep it as a bush and to obtain plenty of glaucous young foliage.

Gray gardens make a tranquil retreat but are best enjoyed on sunny days; rain gives some of the plants a bedraggled look and turns others green, while in winter their appearance is distinctly chilling. For these reasons I would not have a large expanse of gray foliage visible from my windows.

Gold foliage

Golden foliage is cheerful—even on a dull day it suggests sunshine and warmth. A single tree, such as *Gleditsia triacanthos* 'Sunburst' or *Robinia pseudoacacia* 'Frisia,' can light up a whole garden while a tall shrub like the mock orange *Philadelphus coronarius* 'Aureus' will provide just the background for white, blue or orange flowers. In most instances, yellow leaves are at their most brilliant when young and gradually change to green as they age. In the case of the *Robinia*, however, the color becomes more intense, ending up almost orange.

Lonicera nitida 'Baggesen's Gold,' *Choisya ternata* 'Sundance' and *Abelia × grandiflora* 'Francis Mason' are useful mid-height shrubs, while *Spiraea japonica*

Philadelphus coronarius 'Aureus' will lighten up a dark corner and provide contrast or harmony for the flowers of shorter-growing plants. Like other mock oranges it bears white flowers with a delicious and pervasive scent. It should be given a position in part-shade as too much sun causes the leaves to brown along the edges. Here, it is associated with white honesty (Lunaria annua alba).

Berberis thunbergii *'Rose Glow' is here cleverly associated with* Geranium psilostemon, *the pink marbling on the young* Berberis *leaves being picked up and intensified in the strong magenta flowers of the hardy geranium. The gray leaves of the weeping silver pear* (Pyrus salicifolia *'Pendula') cool this rich mixture.*

'Goldflame' and *Berberis thunbergii* 'Aurea,' whose young leaves are so bright as to appear almost luminous, do not grow more than 3 ft. high.

Golden perennials include *Valeriana phu* 'Aurea' which leafs so early that it can be combined with purple and white crocus and forms of both thyme and marjoram. For walls and fences there is the golden hop (*Humulus lupulus* 'Aureus').

All of these plants, with the exception of the trees, are liable to suffer from leaf scorch if planted in full sun especially on dry soils, while in complete shade they turn lime-green. A position where they are shaded at midday suits them best.

Purple foliage

Purple is the term used by gardeners to describe any foliage which consists of a mixture of dark brown and wine-red as in *Cotinus coggygria* 'Royal Purple,' dark bronze as seen in purple fennel and the gray, red and purple of *Salvia officinalis* 'Purpurascens.' Of all colored foliage it most flatters its companions but has the potential to be the most disruptive in the garden.

The safest foliage color to associate with it is gray, the most dangerous is strong yellow, although pale yellow, be it foliage or flower, can be delightful. As a background to white, blue or rose-pink flowers, purple is difficult to beat while red makes a wonderfully rich combination.

The problem with such dark foliage is that it can look heavy and lifeless especially in dull weather, while at a short distance it seems to disappear, leaving a hole in the planting. This is most disconcerting when a large-growing shrub is placed near the front of a border. *Berberis thunbergii* 'Rose Glow' and the smaller-growing 'Harlequin,' in which the young leaves are pink, even if the older ones are dark purple and red, escape this disadvantage.

Where a small purple tree is required, a choice can be made from *Prunus cerasifera* 'Pissardii,' which has pale pink flowers and ruby-red young foliage which darkens later, and the less frequently seen *Prunus virginiana* 'Schubert' whose leaves are green at first and then turn purple-red—an unusual progression. It also has white, star-shaped flowers in spring.

A color scheme of silver and purple

In this border, depicted in late summer when the silver plants are at their best, it is the foliage of silver-gray, blue-gray and purplish tones that brings color, while the main contrasts are provided by the variations of leaf shape and texture.

The large-growing shrubs at the back of this border will take much longer to fill their allotted space than those in the foreground, so, in the meantime, the bare soil around them could be covered by gray-leaved *Stachys byzantina* and *Aurinia saxatilis*, the blue-gray *Acaena adscendens*, or the half-hardy but rapidly spreading *Helichrysum petiolare*. Bulbous alliums with spherical purple flowers, including *A. aflatunense* and *A. christophii*, could be set among the shorter plants for additional interest.

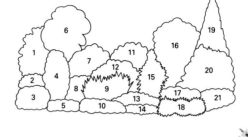

1 *Berberis temolaica*: erect deciduous shrub, 8 ft. tall, with silvery blue leaves, purple-gray stems and pale yellow flowers in spring, followed by red, plum-shaped berries.

2 *Eryngium giganteum*: biennial, growing 2½ ft. tall in its second year, with branching heads of greenish flowers surrounded by a spiky aluminum-gray ruff in summer; once established, a patch will be self-perpetuating.

3 *Senecio cineraria* 'White Diamond': both the deeply lobed leaves and the stems of this 2 ft. tall, slightly tender sub-shrub appear as if they have been cut from white felt; the yellow daisy flowers, which appear in late summer, are often removed in order to maintain the plant's shape.

4 *Foeniculum vulgare* 'Purpureum' (bronze fennel): develops into a clump of ferny, aromatic foliage, 4 ft. tall, with yellow flowers like cow parsley in summer.

5 *Tanacetum densum amani*: dense mats, 6 in. high, are formed from rosettes of tiny leaves like white feathers; a perennial evergreen in mild climates; the groundsel-like flowers are best removed.

6 *Salix exigua*: graceful shrubby willow of suckering habit, 10 ft. tall, with narrow, silky, silver leaves on its arching branches; small catkins appear at the same time as the young leaves in spring.

7 *Rosa glauca*: with its gray-purple leaves and stems, this 6 ft. tall rose is unmistakable and indispensable; pink dog rose flowers are produced in clusters in mid-summer, followed by dark red hips.

8 *Helichrysum splendidum*: rounded evergreen shrub, 2 ft. tall, with short, broad, gray-felted leaves; insignificant yellow daisy flowers can appear at almost any time.

9 *Iris pallida* 'Variegata': 2 ft. tall bearded iris with gray-green, broadly striped with white, leaves; small scented blue flowers are a bonus in early summer.

10 *Sedum* 'Ruby Glow': herbaceous perennial, growing to a height of about 10 in., with succulent, gray leaves on lax, reddish stems; clusters of wine-colored flowers open in late summer or autumn.

11 *Atriplex halimus*: small silvery gray leaves clothe the erect stems of this 6 ft. deciduous shrub; its small flowers are gray.

12 *Berberis thunbergii* 'Rose Glow': the young leaves of this prickly, 5 ft. tall, deciduous shrub are rose-pink, flecked with silver, maturing to plain purple; yellow flowers in spring give rise to tiny red berries.

13 *Hebe pimeleoides* 'Quicksilver': semi-prostrate evergreen shrub, 1 ft. high, with black stems bearing tiny silver-blue leaves and pale lavender flowers which open in midsummer.

14 *Euphorbia myrsinites*: 6 in. tall evergreen perennial, with prostrate stems, waxy

glaucous leaves and green-yellow flowers, which fade to pink, in spring.

15 *Cynara cardunculus*: the large, deeply cut, silver leaves of this herbaceous perennial make impressive clumps from which stout flower stalks spring carrying similar smaller leaves, crowned at 6 ft. with big, blue, thistle-like flowers in late summer.

16 *Cotinus coggygria* 'Grace': 10 ft. tall deciduous shrub with oval, purple-brown leaves; in late summer puffs of pink hairs appear around the flowers.

17 *Artemisia absinthium* 'Lambrook Silver': pale green shoots emerge from a woody base in spring and turn into delicate leaves, 2 ft. high and shaped like those of a carrot but silver-gray; the flowers are tiny yellow bobbles and are best cut off as they fade.

18 *Helictotrichon sempervirens*: evergreen grass with tufts of 1 ft. long, silver-blue leaves; straw-colored, oat-like flowers are produced on 3 ft. stems in summer.

19 *Cupressus glabra*: fast-growing, hardy conifer which will make a 33 ft. tall cone of

blue-gray, scale-like leaves.

20 *Buddleia fallowiana alba*: both the young shoots and leaves of this 6 ft. tall, slightly tender deciduous shrub are silvery but become dark gray with age; fragrant white flowers appear in late summer.

21 *Hebe* 'Red Edge': rounded evergreen shrub, 1½ ft. tall, with a narrow red rim to the gray-green leaves; soft red suffuses the young leaves in spring and summer; the flowers which are produced in midsummer are pink in bud and open white.

Flowering shrubs and perennials

Most of the flower color for winter and early spring will be provided by mahonias and other structural evergreens and by bulbs. If the soil is not of the driest, or the garden is large enough to include a few shrubs which do not have much to recommend them when out of flower, make room for *Lonicera fragrantissima*, a bushy honeysuckle with scented cream flowers which need a dark background for maximum visibility. *Hamamelis × intermedia* 'Pallida' is another winter-scented shrub that I could not live without but it must have maximum shelter and a neutral or acid soil. The delightful Lenten rose (*Helleborus orientalis*) needs cool shade, a retentive soil and lots of manure or compost. *Iris unguicularis*, however, needs the hottest, driest spot you can find.

Once into spring there is no shortage of flowering shrubs. Those hardy old favorites—forsythia, flowering currant (*Ribes sanguineum*) and flowering quince or japonica (*Chaenomeles*)—tolerate a dry soil in cool areas, although growth may be slow and in very dry summers they may defoliate early. My own experience with the spring magnolias is that they will all withstand considerable drought, at least on a sandy soil, and as long as they have shelter from desiccating winds. The most suitable magnolia for small gardens is *M. stellata*, which I like to associate with the dwarf Russian almond (*Prunus tenella* 'Fire Hill'), which has rose-crimson flowers on a miniature thicket of upright stems.

When it comes to brightening the garden, the acid-yellow bracts of the spurges are unrivaled. *Euphorbia characias wulfenii* should be given a prominent position. *Euphorbia × martinii* is a smaller version with a similarly long season, while *E. myrsinites* and *E. rigida* are sprawlers, excellent for trailing over a ledge. *Euphorbia amygdaloides* 'Rubra,' whose dark red young leaves look well with the delicate yellow flowers of *Epimedium perralderianum*, is best in broken shadow, while *E. robbiae* will take dense shade, making first-class ground cover.

Although the common name for Kniphofia is red-hot poker, it is no longer really appropriate as they are now available in a range of colors from cream and yellow to salmon and coral, as well as all the fiery shades, such as the cultivar shown here, 'Bees' Sunset.' Kniphofia also vary greatly in size, the smaller hybrids seeming to do better on dry soils. In winter it is advisable to give the crowns some protection from frost. Because of their strong unusual form, they are best used sparingly, in small groups or even singly.

Lilac time in the dry garden means not the large *Syringa vulgaris* cultivars, although these need not necessarily be excluded if plenty of water can be provided in spring, but compact species with more delicate flowers. *Syringa × persica* grows about 5 ft. tall and has airy clusters of fragrant lilac-colored blooms. The white form 'Alba' is even more attractive. *Syringa × persica laciniata* has deeply segmented leaves and darker lilac flowers. *Syringa meyeri* 'Palibin,' not always recognized as being a lilac, makes a dense rounded shrub only slowly reaching 4 ft. with small leaves and lots of small violet-purple flowers. It is a real charmer!

The most floriferous shrubs for spring are the various members of the broom family but the early shrub roses run them a close second. Some of the wild or near-wild roses tolerate dry sandy soils and *Rosa* 'Canary Bird' is one of the best. It takes up a lot of room but the bright green and fern-like leaves and the single yellow flowers make a splendid sight. The burnet rose (*R. pimpinellifolia*), naturally occurring in sand, was used by the German breeder of the 'Frühlings' group of cultivars. The best known are 'Frühlingsgold,' with big, nearly single, yellow flowers and pervasive scent and 'Frühlingsmorgen,' whose single pink blooms shade to yellow in the center. Both of them grow to a height of at least 6 ft., by as much across. The cranesbill *Geranium* 'Johnson's Blue' makes splendid ground cover under these roses. All the strong-growing *Geranium* will grow in nearly any soil and bulk up rapidly.

By the time summer arrives, there are lots of hardy plants from which to choose: iris, *Anchusa*, poppies, *Armeria*, *Salvia × superba* and *S. haematodes*, *Tradescantia*, *Nepeta*, *Crambe cordifolia*, *Centranthus*, *Linum*, *Centaurea*, so many in fact that I can only describe one or two favorites in any detail. *Papaver spicatum* makes a change from the huge flaunting Oriental poppies, having flowers which are only half the size but in a delightful shade of apricot. *Baptisia australis* is like a thin indigo-blue lupin but with the individual flowers set further apart. It takes time to establish. *Dictamnus albus* also transplants badly. Its flowers, produced on stiff upright stems, are pure white with long curving stamens, or lilac-pink in the variety *purpureus*. The eye-catching seed pods explode

Sedum spectabile 'Brilliant' is not only one of the best herbaceous plants in its own right, attractive at all stages of its development, but it also associates extremely well with other plants of contrasting form or color. Here, it provides an eye-catching base line for Artemisia ludoviciana, a beautiful, though invasive, foliage plant.

when ripe with an audible crack. Like the stems, the seed pods are covered with a citrus-scented oil which in very hot weather is so volatile that a lighted match applied to them on a completely still day will result in a tiny flicker of flame, hence the plant's common name of "burning bush."

There is no shortage of flowering shrubs to combine with these plants. *Kolkwitzia amabilis* 'Pink Cloud' really does cover itself in a cloud of small pink, yellow-throated, funnel-shaped flowers; *Tamarix parviflora* has arching plumes of pink flowers which should be cut back before they turn brown; *Cistus* and *Escallonia* have the advantage of being evergreen, while mock orange (*Philadelphus*) has luminous white flowers that fill the air with one of the strongest perfumes of the year. Probably the best mock orange for dry soils in cool areas is *P. coronarius* but the low-growing *P. microphyllus* is said to tolerate drought better in hot countries.

A garden would hardly seem a garden without roses in midsummer and most of us plant a variety of sorts both old and modern with mixed results. Those in a rich retentive soil with plenty of sun and air will do best. Where drought is mainly due to poor sandy soil, the majority of roses will be under stress and less able to cope with blackspot, mildew and rust—and even an attack of aphids. We are fortunate, therefore, that *Rosa rugosa* actually thrives in a light soil, and doubly fortunate that it is one of the few roses actually worth looking at when not in bloom, while its deliciously scented flowers lead to large, brightly colored hips. Among the "old" roses, *R. × alba* seems to do best on a sandy soil, while the china roses in my experience remain remarkably healthy and free-flowering, although their height is reduced to about half that stated in catalogs.

It has been said that anyone can make a garden colorful in early summer but it takes a dedicated gardener to ensure that it still looks good a month later. This is certainly true of the dry garden, where the lack of moisture is usually most acute from midsummer onward, bringing to a premature end the flowering season of many earlier plants. Yet this is just the time of the year when you would hope to relax in the garden surrounded by color and scent, so room must be found for the following long-flowering

shrubs: *Ceanothus × delileanus* 'Gloire de Versailles' or 'Topaz,' *Ceratostigma willmottianum*, *Spartium*, *Abelia*, *Lavatera* and lots of lavender.

If you do not have room for the 6 ft. wide *Lavatera olbia* 'Rosea' or the prettier 'Barnsley,' try 'Burgundy Wine' which is only half the size and has grayish foliage, or the white 'Ice Cool'—both make a good foreground for buddleia. If you have a large garden and have not yet tried them, consider *Buddleia* 'Pink Delight' whose large flowers are a clean bright color, or 'Dartmoor' in which the rich purple flowers come in enormous flat panicles instead of the usual curving spikes. Far better for small gardens are *B. davidii* 'Nanho Blue' ('Petite Indigo') and 'Nanho Purple' ('Petite Plum') which grow only 5 ft. high by as much wide and whose flowers are produced at the end of slender arching branches.

Lavatera, the tree mallow, is the perfect present for an impatient gardener. From a rooted cutting it will grow to a height and width of at least 5 ft. in two seasons, sometimes even in the first, and flowers non-stop for as much as four months. The cultivar illustrated here is 'Bredon Springs,' a particularly good form.

Indigofera gerardiana, Hedysarum multijugum and *Lespedeza thunbergii* are sun-loving members of the pea family which can be treated rather like herbaceous plants and pruned almost to the ground every spring. Their purple and pink flowers look well when associated with the fluffy soft blue flowers of *Caryopteris × clandonensis* or its much darker form 'Kew Blue,' and against the arching flower sprays of *Tamarix ramosissima* 'Pink Cascade.' This late tamarisk has beautiful glaucous foliage and can be either hard pruned in spring or allowed to grow into a rather gaunt little tree.

Among herbaceous perennials flowering in the latter half of summer, *Agapanthus* and *Kniphofia* are outstanding although they need a rich soil as well as good drainage and in very cold areas some protection, at least until established. *Penstemon*, the delightful airy *Diascia* in varying shades of pink, and two South African daisies, *Osteospermum jucundum* (magenta-pink) and *O. ecklonis* (dazzling white), all have long flowering seasons and, although unreliably hardy, are certainly worth a try.

In the yellow, orange and red range, *Achillea, Anthemis, Oenothera, Coreopsis, Rudbeckia* and the daylily *(Hemerocallis)* are easy-going, although it always seems odd that the daylily, which looks so appropriate and happy near water, can do remarkably well on dry soils—and it does even better given some shade and irrigation when in flower. The thistle-like *Eryngium* and *Echinops* seem much more appropriate to an arid soil, as do the papery flowers of *Catananche* and the moisture-storing leaves of *Sedum spectabile* whose rich brown seed heads will remain to provide interest as autumn drifts into winter.

This mixture of self-seeders is ideal when a cottagey effect is desired. However, the acid-yellow Alchemilla mollis *can become a weed unless controlled and sea holly* (Eryngium) *needs eradicating before it has made a deep tap root. On the other hand,* Lychnis coronaria *is easily pulled up if in the wrong place, and lavender—here* Lavandula angustifolia *'Hidcote'—is less free with its seedlings.*

Annuals, biennials and half-hardy perennials

There is certainly no other class of plant which provides color over such a long period as half-hardy bedding and it may be the ideal solution for a small flower bed or a terrace, but the plants need not be set out in regimented rows, nor need their colors be harsh. It is now possible to assemble plants whose colors harmonize rather than contrast. Among the most drought-resistant bedding plants are pelargoniums, *Cineraria maritima*, petunias, French and African marigolds *(Tagetes)*, zinnias and fibrous begonias which tolerate partial shade.

The growing interest in container gardening has resulted in the increasing availability of half-hardy plants which have to be propagated from cuttings. Often found under the heading of "patio plants" are the daisy-flowered *Argyranthemum*, *Osteospermum* and *Bidens ferulifolia*, silver-leaved gazanias, verbenas like *V.* 'Silver Anne' and 'Sissinghurst' and the wandering gray-leaved *Helichrysum petiolare*, all of which produce quick results and are excellent for dry conditions. In particular, they are useful for filling those unexpected gaps which occur even in the best organized gardens. If you have a frost-free greenhouse, you can take cuttings and over-winter them.

Also useful for filling midsummer gaps, annuals can be used in new gardens or beds to cover bare soil while trees and shrubs are growing. In spring, try sowing Virginian stock *(Malcolmia maritima)*, night-scented stock *(Matthiola)*, nasturtium, echium, toadflax *(Linaria)*, annual poppies *(Papaver)*, love-in-a-mist *(Nigella damascens)*, crimson flax *(Linum grandiflorum rubrum)*, cornflower *(Centaurea cyanus)*, and clary *(Salvia)* or star of the veldt *(Dimorphotheca)*, in the position you wish them to flower. Given warm weather, flowering should start in the late summer and last until the first frosts, but you will need to hand weed and thin them. Remember, however, as in the desert, moisture is needed for germination and establishment. Tobacco plants *(Nicotiana)* and *Lavatera trimestris* 'Mont Blanc' and 'Silver Cup' are useful as they are taller, but must be purchased as young plants or raised in a heated greenhouse.

Many of the best annuals that are suitable for growing in dry soils have, by nature, a short flowering season and although plant breeders have produced selections in which this is extended, regular dead-heading to prevent the production of seed is still worthwhile in the case of certain plants. These include African daisy *(Arctotis)*, prickly poppy *(Argemone)*, marigold *(Calendula)*, cornflower *(Centaurea)*, Palm Springs daisy *(Cladanthus)*, morning glory *(Convolvulus)* and Californian poppy *(Eschscholzia)*.

An alternative to annuals is to sow biennials, such as foxgloves *(Digitalis)*, sweet Williams *(Dianthus barbatus)*, variegated honesty *(Lunaria)*, sweet rocket *(Hesperis matronalis)* or *Verbascum bombyciferum*. Biennials produce only stems, roots and leaves in the first year and will not flower until the following year, after which most of them will die, leaving behind self-sown seedlings to be pulled out, transplanted or left, depending on where they have chosen to grow.

Whichever plants you choose to use as temporary fillers in the dry garden, make sure that they do not put your permanent shrubs and plants at risk by depriving them of moisture or light.

This tapestry of annuals contains many childhood favorites. There are daisy-shaped marigolds (Calendula officinalis), nasturtiums (Tropaeolum) whose seeds can be pickled as a substitute for capers, the handsome seed pods of love-in-a-mist (Nigella) and the silky heads of squirrel tail grass (Hordeum jubatum).

Bulbs

Most bulbs come prepacked to cope with drought, the exception being those which flower during the height of summer such as lilies, *Galtonia*, *Camassia*, *Schizostylis*, *Crinum* and some gladioli. Many of these are native to countries where winters are dry and cold and the summers hot and wet, but they may be worth a try if your soil is retentive or you can water once a week when the weather is very hot and dry.

The bulb season in the dry garden could be said to begin when the buds of *Amaryllis belladonna* push through bare soil in late summer—their leaves follow later—and open to large white-throated pink trumpets. *Amaryllis* needs a warm spot under a wall. *Nerine bowdenii* should be given a similar position except in mild areas. Its spidery rose-pink trumpets appear in autumn. Again these are bereft of leaves which have died off earlier creating an unwelcome gap. My way of dealing with this is to plant winter-flowering pansies between the bulbs when the leaves turn yellow. The bright yellow *Sternbergia* is another sun-loving autumn bulb.

Between the flowering of the amaryllis and nerines is *Colchicum* time. The big, pure white goblets of *C. speciosum* 'Album' look superb against purple *Cotinus* whose leaves at this time are almost black. I prefer to use those with mauve flowers among silver plants.

The true autumn crocus (*Crocus speciosus*) flowers later and looks best naturalized in grass, as do so many of the stronger spring bulbs like daffodils. My own garden is too small to have an area of rough grass so the delightful miniature crocus of winter and spring along with dwarf iris, scillas, *Chionodoxa* and the rich blue × *Chionoscilla allenii* are planted in clumps at the front of borders, between aubrieta, marjoram, hardy geraniums and the like. Snowdrops and winter aconites co-exist with a big patch of *Vinca minor* under a tree, daffodils are planted among daylilies (*Hemerocallis*) whose developing foliage hides that of the narcissi, and *Anemone blanda* makes a brilliant carpet of color under the skirts of deciduous shrubs. The leaves of *Tristagma* (syn. *Ipheion*) *uniflorum* appear in autumn although it does not flower until spring, so I use this as a foreground to a bed of wallflowers. Their leaves clothe the soil for at least seven months and their star-shaped blue flowers coincide with those of the wallflowers.

Tulips have a reputation for rapidly fading away unless lifted, dried and correctly stored, but in a dry, sunny garden I find the large-flowered cultivars as well as the stripy-leaved dwarf *Tulipa kaufmanniana* and *T. greigii* hybrids will often continue to flower for many years when left in the ground, although the flowers do diminish in size. Tulips look particularly well growing among herbaceous perennials where they provide color before the majority of the plants re-emerge. You do need to plant them in tight groups, however, and mark their positions or later some of them will end up speared by a garden fork!

The ornamental onions might also have been made for the dry garden. There are lots to choose from but some can become a nuisance especially on light soils. *Allium aflatuense*, *A. karataviense*, *A. cernuum*, *A. caeruleum* and *A. siculum* are attractive and safe. The most outstanding is *A. christophii*, its great, airy, lilac globes on stiff 2 ft. stems which look their best floating over low perennials before a backdrop of pink and crimson roses.

LEFT *As the shoots of crown imperial (Fritillaria imperialis 'Lutea') emerge in early spring, they will let you know of their presence by their curious smell, although little of it remains when they flower six weeks or so later. Available in shades of orange as well as yellow, these bulbs need a sunny spot and well-prepared soil. According to legend their bells originally faced outward until they saw Christ on His way to Calvary. Certainly if you turn up a bell, you will find a teardrop at the base of every nectary.*

A *five-into-one border*

Designed for a sunny spot in the garden, this colorful flower border, shown here in early summer, is made up of five small groups, each containing a large-growing flowering shrub and three smaller shrubs or perennials. Where there is not room for a large flower bed, a smaller plant group, such as any of the five illustrated here, may be useful. With a few exceptions, which are noted in the descriptions, all the shrubs are deciduous, and the border would look best if set against a backdrop of tall evergreens or planted in front of a wall or fence on which evergreens, such as *Garrya elliptica*, *Ceanothus* and *Pyracantha*, could be trained.

A: Three shrubs to provide color over a long period with an ornamental grass for contrast of form.

A1 *Kolkwitzia amabilis* 'Pink Cloud': known as the "beauty bush" from its appearance in early summer when its arching branches are massed with small, bell-shaped flowers which are pink with a yellow throat; its mid-green leaves sometimes turn red in autumn; grows to 6 ft.

A2 *Potentilla fruticosa* 'Abbotswood': bushy shrub, which will grow to 3 ft., with small grayish leaves and white flowers, produced almost continuously from late spring to early autumn.

A3 *Lavandula angustifolia* 'Hidcote': dense purple-blue flowers are produced in profusion in late summer on this compact, 1½ ft. tall, gray-green-leaved shrub.

A4 *Miscanthus sinensis* 'Variegatus': 5 ft. tall, ornamental deciduous grass, with arching leaves, striped cream and green.

B: A small group that will provide interest in autumn

B1 *Clerodendrum trichotomum*: open-branched and large-leaved, this 10 ft. tall, tree-like shrub produces clusters of scented white flowers in late summer, followed by turquoise berries on crimson calyces.

B2 *Ceanothus × delileanus* 'Topaz': 6 ft. tall, rounded shrub with mid-green leaves and panicles of bright blue flowers in late summer and autumn.

B3 *Ballota pseudodictamnus*: somewhat sprawling in habit, this 2 ft. tall evergreen subshrub has rounded gray leaves on felted white stems; tiny mauve flowers appear in midsummer.

B4 *Liatris spicata* 'Kobold': 2 ft. tall herbaceous perennial; the foliage makes a grassy rosette from which the truncheon-shaped flower spike, encircled with fluffy rose-purple blooms, rises in late summer.

C: Berberis provides a strong accent in this delightful, scented group for summer color.

C1 *Cytisus battandieri*: fast-growing shrub of erect habit, 10 ft. tall, with trifoliate leaves covered in a gray-green, satin-like down; tight clusters of pineapple-scented yellow flowers appear in early summer.

C2 *Berberis thunbergii atropurpurea*: foliage shrub, 6 ft. tall, with small reddish-brown leaves turning rich red in autumn; it has small yellow flowers in spring and red berries which last into winter.

C3 *Rosa pimpinellifolia* double white: 5 ft. tall burnet rose; small, sweetly scented, globe-shaped flowers in early summer.

C4 *Iris* 'Blue Shimmer': 2½ ft. tall bearded iris with large, scented flowers, which have delicate blue stippling on a clean white ground, in early summer.

D: A well-balanced group providing interest from spring through to autumn.

D1 *Cotoneaster franchetii*: sage-green leaves with a silvery reverse clothe the arching branches of this 10 ft. tall semi-evergreen shrub; in autumn it carries masses of orange, pear-shaped berries.
D2 *Prunus tenella* 'Fire Hill' (Russian almond): bushy shrub which develops a thicket of slender stems, each one wreathed in dainty, single, rose-crimson flowers in spring; small, glossy, willow-like leaves follow; will eventually grow to 4 ft.
D3 *Achillea* 'Moonshine': 2 ft. tall herbaceous perennial with gray-green, fronded foliage from which flat heads of clear yellow flowers rise throughout summer.
D4 *Salvia × sylvestris* 'Mainacht' ('May Night'): sage-like leaves with clustered spikes of violet-blue flowers are produced over many weeks starting in early summer; will grow to 1½ ft. tall.

E: A combination of soft-colored flowers and handsome foliage.

E1 *Lavatera* 'Barnsley': vigorous and fast-growing sub-shrub, 6 ft. tall; grayish leaves and pale pink, chalice-shaped flowers from midsummer until stopped by frost.
E2 *Perovskia* 'Blue Spire': this 4 ft. tall sub-shrub is well named—its silvery stems are topped in late summer with lavender-blue, nepeta-like flowers; its gray leaves are deeply toothed and smell of sage.
E3 *Eryngium × tripartitum*: 2 ft. herbaceous perennial with large branching sprays of small teasel-like blue cones and bracts in midsummer.
E4 *Crambe maritima* (sea kale): herbaceous perennial, growing to 2 ft. tall, with large, glaucous, waxen leaves; a cloud of white scented flowers is produced in midsummer.

THROUGH THE SEASONS

Work in the garden cannot be governed by dates on the calendar. Early spring, which tomorrow may turn into winter again, and late spring, when the danger of frost is all but over, will offer quite different appearances in the garden and will differ again according to where you live. How far you are above sea level, the proximity of hills or even whether your garden is an urban one will determine when you should plant or prune, propagate or protect.

Early summer in an English garden but one which has clearly sought inspiration from Mediterranean examples. Although the flowers of Cistus *'Silver Pink,'* Helianthemum *'Red Orient' and orange 'Henfield Brilliant,' backed by a dark bearded iris and the yellow spikes of* Asphodeline, *will last only a few weeks, clematis seed heads on the wall prove that spring did not lack color. In the well-planned garden every season will bring its pleasures but also its essential tasks.*

Early spring

Snowdrops *(Galanthus)* and winter aconites *(Eranthis hyemalis)* may appear in late winter but before they have faded, other dwarf bulbs —crocuses, scillas, *Chionodoxa, Anemone blanda* and *Triteleia*—provide bright patches of floral optimism. *Iris reticulata* and grape hyacinths *(Muscari)* follow and the scent of hyacinths and crown imperials fills the air. The true heralds of spring are daffodils but as we enjoy the early cyclamineus hybrids, the first kaufmanniana hybrid tulips appear, in brilliant mixtures of red and yellow, orange or pink and white.

Spring is the most favored season for the dry garden; winter rains should have replenished its soil reservoirs and the sun is warm enough to make the crozier-shaped heads of *Euphorbia characias wulfenii* display their lime-yellow bracts against the blue flowers of rosemary. In more shady spots, the cream-veined, arrow-shaped leaves of *Arum italicum italicum* combine with the dark green foliage and apple-green flowers of *Helleborus foetidus* and lavender-blue periwinkle *(Vinca)*. The pink flowers of almond trees appear and on *Prunus padus* 'Grandiflora' the finger-shaped clusters of fragrant white flowers accompany the gray-backed leaves.

Trees and shrubs

● Finish planting hardy shrubs. Check newly planted shrubs after frost and gales; if the roots have lifted, tread the soil firm.
● Prune *Buddleia davidii, Caryopteris*, deciduous ceanothus, *Ceratostigma, Cotinus coggygria* 'Atropurpurea,' *Elsholtzia, Lespedeza, Indigofera, Perovskia, Hedysarum, Spiraea japonica, Tamarix gallica* and *T. ramosissima*, cutting back the shoots from the previous year to within two or three buds of the older wood.
● Roses not pruned in summer or autumn should receive attention. *Rosa pimpinellifolia* and *R. nitida* need only a light trim. Remove dead

Crocus tommasianus *opens its flowers to the cool sunshine of early spring.*

and sickly growth from the mature bushes of *R. rugosa* and *R. glauca* and cut out some of the old wood that has ceased to flower freely.
● Trim dead flowerheads off summer heathers.

Climbers and wall shrubs

● Cut back flowering shoots of winter jasmine to one or two buds. Shorten the strong, young shoots to keep the plant within bounds.
● Thin out summer jasmine, removing completely some of the older shoots.
● Cut down each stem of later flowering clematis to the lowest pair of strong buds.
● Shorten the previous summer's growth of evergreen ceanothus that flower on the current season's wood to about 4 in.
● Sow seeds of annual climbers in a greenhouse, cold frame or on a sunny windowsill.

Hedges

● Plant evergreens, such as box, *Euonymus*, laurel, holly and yew.

Perennials

● Remove any dead stalks remaining from autumn.
● Lift, divide and replant congested clumps of late-flowering plants, adding compost or manure.
● In areas where winters are severe, plant new purchases, including ornamental grasses.
● Cut back non-evergreen grasses almost to ground level. "Comb out" dead blades from *Helictotrichon sempervirens* and *Festuca* grasses.

Annuals and biennials

● Toward the end of this period prepare the ground (see page 40) and sow hardy annuals if you did not do so in the autumn.
● Sow seeds of tender plants under glass.

Bulbs

● Lift, divide and replant snowdrops if they are overcrowded or you wish to increase your stock.
● Feed all visible bulbs with a top-dressing of bonemeal or spray the leaves with a foliar feed.
● Plant cyclamen, nerines, amaryllis and alliums.

Lawns

● Start mowing regularly if the weather permits.
● Apply mosskiller if necessary.
● Toward the end of the period apply a spring/summer fertilizer.

Irrigation

● Check that irrigation systems work efficiently. On drip systems remove the end caps and flush the main and lateral pipes.

General

● Apply a herbicide to gravel drives and paths.
● Remove algae and moss from paving with tar oil, a commercial product or household bleach. Brush timber decking with a stiff yard broom

dipped in a solution of household bleach, following the manufacturer's instructions.

● Remove weed seedlings from all beds and borders; on poor soils apply a slow-acting fertilizer and hoe in.

● As soon as light soils have warmed but are still moist, apply a mulch of a minimum 2 in. thickness to all bare soil but do not pile it against the stems of trees and shrubs. Top off existing mulches where they are thinning.

Late spring

With every passing day the garden palette becomes richer. Purple aubrieta, yellow alyssum and white candytuft carpet the ground. Mauve or white wisteria, deep blue ceanothus or *Fremontodendron* starred with yellow, mallow-like flowers drape walls. A rose-purple cloud envelops the Judas tree while laburnum droops golden chains. Brilliantly yellow, too, are the single flowers of *Rosa* 'Canary Bird' and the profusion of pea-like flowers of brooms. Developing foliage adds to the kaleidoscope, with *Spiraea japonica* 'Goldflame' offering tan and buff, *Berberis thunbergii* 'Darts Red Lady' copper, and *Photinia × fraseri* crimson.

The new shoots of herbaceous plants like *Sedum spectabile*, daylilies *(Hemerocallis)* and Japanese anemones *(Anemone hupehensis)* help to disguise the untidy leaves of early-flowering bulbs. The air is full of scent: *Berberis, Pyracantha rogersiana*, sweet rocket *(Hesperis matronalis)* and vanilla-scented *Azara microphylla* all contribute but none is so evocative as box *(Buxus)* hedging in flower.

Trees and shrubs
● Plant shrubs that are not fully hardy.
● Water recently planted trees and shrubs; spray the branches if the weather is dry.
● Hard prune *Ballota, Helichrysum splendidum, Senecio cineraria, Santolina* and shrubby

Purple Allium aflatunense, *yellow* Euphorbia characias wulfenii *and* Galactites tomentosa.

artemisias by removing most of the previous year's growth. Lightly trim *Helichrysum italicum*. Prune *Romneya* either cutting to living wood or to ground level. On *Spartium junceum*, cut back the previous year's growth to within 1–2 in. of the older wood.

● Prune forsythias and *Ribes* immediately after flowering, removing approximately a quarter of the oldest stems.

● Cut out any dead or diseased wood from evergreens and shape the bushes if necessary.

● Trim lavender and winter heathers.

● Spray susceptible rose bushes regularly with a combined insecticide and fungicide, adding a foliar feed to the spray if your soil is poor.

Climbers and wall shrubs
● If spring-flowering clematis have filled their allotted space, cut the stems that have flowered almost to their base and remove dead and weak shoots; if they threaten to take over the garden, cut them to within 3 ft. of the base but feed and

keep watered. Prune *Garrya* and *Acacia* to shape. Clip ivy back to the face of the wall.

● Watch roses and honeysuckles for aphids and spray with an appropriate insecticide.

● Climbers on walls may need watering.

Hedges
● Evergreen hedges that were not clipped to shape in summer and need to be severely reduced in size are best dealt with now. Feed and keep watered.

Perennials
● Support weak-stemmed and tall plants.

Annuals and biennials
● Sow seed of biennials such as honesty, verbascum and foxgloves.
● When the danger of frost is over, plant out half-hardy bedding subjects.

Bulbs
● Remove faded flowerheads from daffodils and tulips but leave stems and foliage intact.

Lawns
● Rake to remove dead grass and moss. Aerate the soil by slitting and spiking, and top-dress the lawn (see page 45 and also under "Autumn").

Irrigation
● Some watering may be advisable on sandy soils which have not been mulched, especially if there are drying winds.

General
● Remove weeds, particularly perennials which need to be dug out or treated with a herbicide.
● Mulch heavy soils once the soil has warmed, and also light, sandy soils if you did not do so in early spring. Water the ground first if it is dry.

Early summer

As spring's emerging greenness unfurls into the full leafy banner of summer, the soil is no longer visible. Although the sun has nearly reached its zenith, everything is still delightfully fresh and tender. The pale lavender blooms of *Abutilon vitifolium* are set among downy gray leaves; *Cistus* and poppy *(Papaver)* petals are the texture of silk; the mallow-like flowers of *Fremontodendron* may be of a brassy shade but its stems and the underside of its leaves are coated in a rich brown felt; even the sharp Christmas holly *(Ilex aquifolium)* has produced soft young leaves.

The rose season has started in earnest, the *rugosa* roses having followed close on the heels of *R. pimpinellifolia*, their rich scent joining those of flag irises and musk pinks like the old-fashioned *Dianthus* 'Mrs. Sinkins.' Soon will come the even more powerful aroma of mock orange *(Philadelphus)* and honeysuckle *(Lonicera)* to fill the air.

On a sunny wall, the purple-blue flowers of *Solanum crispum* make an ideal partnership with *Robinia hispida* and form a backdrop for the massed pink trumpets of *Koelreuteria*.

Most of the hardy plants that flowered earlier in the year appreciate dappled shade but now we have the real sun lovers: the burning bush *(Dictamnus albus)* with its pure white flowers, pale blue flaxes *(Linum)*, lupins, thrift *(Armeria maritima)* and *Crambe cordifolia* with immense, airy flowerheads of small white flowers.

Rock roses *(Helianthemum)*, spilling on to paving or over low walls, provide pools of brilliant color, except on dull days when their flowers stay tightly shut. Hardy geraniums and *Alchemilla mollis* flower in both sun and shade, and make excellent ground cover.

Trees and shrubs
- Prune spring-flowering spireas by cutting

Cistus × purpureus *fills this summer garden with vibrant color.*

flowering shoots back to the first strong new shoot. *Buddleia alternifolia* and *Escallonia* should be pruned immediately after they have flowered. This is done by removing approximately one third of the branches. Lightly trim rosemary, brooms and dwarf *Genista* also after flowering but do not cut hard into the old wood. You should also shorten the flowered shoots of *Teucrium fruticans*.
- Dead-head lilacs and repeat-flowering roses.
- Softwood cuttings can be taken of shrubs like *Caryopteris*, *Cotinus*, hebes, lavender, rosemary and *Santolina*.
- Water newly planted subjects, especially trees, as necessary.

Climbers and wall shrubs
- Plant out annual climbers.
- Prune the ceanothus which have already flowered, cutting back shoots that are growing away from the wall or maybe crowding other plants to about 4 in.
- Shorten the young shoots of *Chaenomeles* and *Pyracantha* that are growing away from the wall to three or four buds.
- Dead-head repeat-flowering roses.
- Tie in the new shoots of climbers, such as roses, while they are still young and pliable.

Hedges
- Trim box hedges.

Perennials
- Dead-head early flowering kinds, particularly those whose seedlings may be a problem.
- Continue staking and tying tall-growing plants.
- Cut back aubrietas, arabis and helianthemums by at least one third as soon as flowering is over.
- On a reserve plot sow seeds of hollyhocks, sweet rocket, lupins and other hardy perennials.
- Take cuttings of pinks, using non-flowering side shoots; root them in pots in rooting compost or in a sand-lined trench.

Bulbs
- Cut rough grass containing naturalized bulbs as soon as the bulb foliage turns brown.

Lawns
- Mow and edge your lawn regularly. This should be done as often as once or twice a week if the grass is growing strongly.
- If there is a dry spell, either water the grass or raise the blades on the mower and reduce the frequency of mowing.

Irrigation
- Whether water is being applied regularly to the garden or only during dry spells, your irrigation system needs to be monitored and any problems dealt with as quickly as possible. If you have an underground pipe system, check all

the sprinklers routinely and keep an eye open for leaks and uneven watering. With drip irrigation make certain the filter is clean and that the emitters are working. If they get blocked, clean them or replace with new.

General
● Continue the onslaught on weeds.

Late summer

With the sun burning brighter and the air daily becoming drier, this is the time for the family to move outdoors—to eat, to play, to read. Summer greenery is profuse, the garden feels more enclosed, more private, smaller. Trees cast dappled shadows, providing welcome shade. New growth has ceased on most trees and many appear heavy and dull, yet the pinnate leaves of *Robinia*, *Gleditsia* and *Sophora* retain their lightness and elegance, while to these qualities *Koelreuteria paniculata* now adds panicles of yellow blossom.

These are usually the driest weeks of the year and watering restrictions may come into force. Now all the earlier labors undertaken to improve the soil and spread mulches are paying off, while those plants which thrive on heat and drought luxuriate in the conditions they love best. The lawn may be the color of straw but the flowers of *Perovskia* have taken on a richer shade of blue, and the silver leaves of *Artemisia* and *Senecio* have turned almost white.

It is no longer necessary to brush against plants such as lavender, marjoram or the curry plant (*Helichrysum angustifolium*) in order to enjoy their fragrance, for they will release it freely into the hot air of midday. Toward evening, the spires of creamy bells produced by spiky yuccas exude the smell of lemons, and as darkness falls the even stronger perfumes of tobacco plants (*Nicotiana*) and night-scented stock (*Matthiola bicornis*) fill the garden.

The hot colors of Crocosmia, *dahlias and* Kniphofia *are appropriate for late summer.*

Many stalwarts of the herbaceous border may stop flowering at this point, but this is the time when half-hardy plants and annuals which originate in hotter countries come to our rescue. Pelargoniums, mesembryanthemums, marigolds, petunias, *Eschscholzia* and zinnias, whether they are used for massed planting or to fill gaps in mixed borders, provide a rich display of color and interesting flower shapes.

Trees and shrubs
● Prune *Philadelphus*, *Tamarix tetrandra* and once-flowering shrub roses which do not bear hips. Remove about a quarter of the oldest stems and shorten back branches which have flowered. Lightly trim *Cistus*.

Climbers and wall shrubs
● Rambler roses need pruning after they flower. Basically, this entails removing the old canes and tying in the new. However, as some cultivars do not produce sufficient new wood, you may need to retain some of the old wood as well. It will also be necessary to shorten the laterals on wisteria to four or five leaves.

Hedges
● Trim yew and holly hedges.

Herbaceous plants
● Lift, divide and replant bearded iris at three-year intervals. You should also improve the quality of the soil by adding both compost and bonemeal. Re-use only the outer parts of the rhizomes. Then cut away half the leaf and water them until they have re-established.
● *Alchemilla* and hardy geraniums are best cut to the ground as soon as flowering is over. If watered, they should rapidly produce new foliage and, in the case of some geraniums, more flowers as well.

Annuals and biennials
● Regular dead-heading will encourage more flowers and extend the season of interest of these plants. Tired and straggly plants may respond if cut back, fertilized and watered.

Lawns
● This is the best time to prepare the ground for the establishment of a new lawn. The ground should be ready for seeding or sodding as soon as the soil is moist enough.

Irrigation
● Continue to check that any irrigation system that you have installed is working efficiently and not wasting water.

General
● With less horticultural maintenance at this time of the year, there may be opportunities to tackle construction jobs such as repairs to paving and painting wooden surfaces or treating them with a preservative.

Autumn

The mellow late-afternoon autumn sun intensifies the crimson, scarlet and orange of Virginia creeper (*Parthenocissus quinquefolia*), *Berberis thunbergii* and *Cotinus coggygria* and other foliage. Ornamental grasses now make their greatest impact. All summer their thin leaves and fountain-like form have provided increasing contrast for the rounder shapes of shrubs, but now many add their flowers and none more dramatically than pampas grass (*Cortaderia selloana*), especially when its great silver plumes are seen against the brilliant foliage of *Crataegus persimilis* 'Prunifolia' or some other autumn-coloring tree.

Many autumn flowers—*Aster × frikartii*, *Lavatera*, *Ceratostigma*, *Abelia* and the late ceanothus—made their main display at the end of summer but now they are joined by the blue flowers of *Caryopteris* and flat heads of sedum.

This is the season of harvest all over the garden. The *rugosa* and *glauca* roses are heavy with hips; the turquoise-blue berries of *Clerodendrum trichotomum* hang in clusters, while the coral-shaded fruits of *Berberis* 'Rubrostilla' are almost translucent. Crocus-shaped colchicums and yellow sternbergias are succeeded by the true autumn crocuses, *Cyclamen hederifolium* and the frilly pink trumpets of *Nerine bowdenii*, while *Elaeagnus × ebbingei* provides one of the sweetest fragrances of the year.

Helichrysum bracteatum, *Helipterum roseum*, yarrow and statice (*Limonium*) can be hung until dry and then arranged with the heads of ornamental onions (*Allium*) and grasses like *Stipa gigantea*. Before autumn has given way to winter, many so-called winter-flowering shrubs, like *Jasminum nudiflorum*, *Mahonia × media* and *Viburnum farreri*, are in bloom.

Autumn is a good time to consider each part of the garden and decide if changes are needed in the overall design or the choice of plants.

Cotoneaster, Berberis *and* Cotinus coggygria *provide autumnal berries and leaf color.*

Trees and shrubs

- For light soils, plant hardy subjects in early autumn and more tender ones in spring.
- Propagate deciduous berberis and ceanothus, hebes, lavenders, potentillas and *Viburnum tinus* from cuttings rooted in a greenhouse in early autumn. Other woody shrubs such as box and spiraeas will root outdoors from hardwood cuttings taken a month later.

Climbers and wall shrubs

- Prune repeat-flowering roses. Remove dead and weak stems and cut back shoots that have produced flowers to about 6 in. If the rose is too tall, prune the leaders to a good bud.
- Secure climbers before the winter gales.

Hedges

- Trim formal deciduous hedges.

Perennials

- If you like a tidy garden, cut down dead top growth. Do not prune evergreen grasses.
- Plant new purchases in mild areas. Lift, split up and replant early- and summer-flowering plants which you may want to increase or which have become overcrowded.

Annuals and biennials

- Lift tender plants such as pelargoniums and *Osteospermum* and winter them under glass.
- Biennial plants like wallflowers, foxgloves and Scotch thistle (*Onopordum acanthium*) should be purchased now or, if grown from seed, moved to their flowering positions.

Bulbs

- Plant spring-flowering bulbs as early as possible. Leave tulips until late autumn.

Lawns

- Grass that was allowed to grow longer in the summer because of heat and drought can be cut shorter again. As winter approaches, mow less often and raise the blades again.
- On poor soils apply an autumn/winter fertilizer that is low in nitrogen and high in phosphorus and potassium.
- Scarify, aerate and top-dress to reduce compaction and encourage deep rooting (see also under "Late spring").

Irrigation

- Drain water from drip irrigation systems.
- Lag stand pipes.

General

- Add fallen leaves to the compost heap, or place them in a container to form leaf mold or reserve them for protecting tender plants.
- Vacant ground can be dug and manured if the soil is heavy. Dress with lime if you wish to raise the pH and improve the structure of the soil. Leave the surface rough and exposed to the action of frosts.

Winter

The importance of good garden design becomes very apparent. This is the season when we most appreciate the woody plants—both deciduous and evergreen—particularly when a hoarfrost etches every twig and leaf in silver. While bare trees and shrubs create "lines" in the winter scene, the evergreens provide volume, mass and texture. The solid forms and glossy leaves of *Mahonia*, *Pittosporum* and *Aucuba* hold center stage, supported in turn by ground-covering ivies, *Euonymus*, periwinkle *(Vinca)* and the bold leaves of bergenia, green in shade, but the color of beetroot in full sun.

Although the weather may not encourage us to linger, this is the time to enjoy the shiny, mahogany-colored bark of *Prunus serrula* and the creamy pink trunk of *Betula ermanii*, particularly in the fragile winter sunshine, as well as bushes bright with red berries, holly and cotoneaster and fistfuls of black-eyed scarlet berries on *Pyracantha* 'Watereri.'

There can be fragrant surprises, too—the tiny, yellow, bell-shaped flowers of *Mahonia japonica*, reminiscent in both form and perfume of lily-of-the-valley, and the heavy, honey-like scent given off by the insignificant creamy flowers of a *Sarcococca*. Best of all is the unmistakable fragrance of wintersweet *(Chimonanthus praecox)*. A few sprigs of its curious, waxy yellow flowers will be sufficient to scent a whole room, and it is perhaps indoors that the beautifully marked, sweetly fragrant lavender-blue *Iris unguicularis* from Algeria can best be enjoyed. Bring in the flowers while they are still tightly furled and watch the petals expand and to encourage the plant to produce still more.

Unless your garden is under snow or in the grip of frost, there is always a small amount of tidying, pruning or mulching to be done, perhaps some planting too. If your soil is heavy clay, keep off it when it is wet, but a light,

Hoarfrost gives standard honeysuckles a second season of beauty in winter.

sandy soil comes to no harm if worked in winter. While rain in winter may not seem of much use to plants, with the exception of evergreens and conifers, it is vital for building up the moisture content of soil in preparation for spring and the renewal of growth.

Trees and shrubs

- Plants with bare roots—mostly trees and roses—should be planted as long as the ground is not frozen or snow-covered. Stake trees and make a shallow saucer shape around the trunk to retain water when irrigating by hand.
- Protect evergreen shrubs which are on the borderline of hardiness for your area, such as *Cistus*. Pack straw or dry leaves among small plants, securing it in place with burlap fixed to canes, pruned conifer branches or hedge trimmings. Large shrubs and hedges are best protected by wattle hurdles or plastic windbreak mesh secured to tall stakes and positioned to give shelter both from the prevailing wind and

winter sun. For plants whose roots are liable to suffer from frost, such as *Ceratostigma* and *Romneya*, apply a deep mulch of bracken fern or fallen leaves held in place with netting.
- Knock snow off upright conifers and hedges.

Climbers and wall shrubs

- Protect tender plants like myrtle and ceanothus with a "quilt" of leaves, straw or fiberglass insulation sandwiched between netting against the wall and attached to vine eyes.
- Prune wisteria to within 3 in. of the old wood, except shoots needed for extension.
- *Parthenocissus* which are grown on the walls of the house may need light trimming and cutting back from windows and eaves. Ornamental grape vines which have filled their allotted space should have all their young shoots cut back to one or two buds.
- Check plant supports and extend wires or trellis, where necessary.

Herbaceous plants

- Protect the crowns of tender plants with leaves or bracken. Alpines with silver or hairy leaves dislike winter wet so they should be protected with a sheet of glass or clear plastic supported on bricks.

Bulbs

- If bulbs are grown in flower beds and not in grass, remove weeds and mulch well.

Lawns

- Remove fallen leaves but avoid walking on the grass in frosty weather. In mild areas, mow once or twice with the blades set high.
- Mix a top-dressing of soil, peat and sand ready to apply in the spring (see page 45).

General

- Send garden machinery, mower, pruning shears, and so on for servicing or sharpening.

KEY PLANTS FOR THE DRY GARDEN

In spite of the constraints, there are so many desirable plants which grow in dry soils that, making a choice can prove difficult. To help you establish a varied framework in a new garden or select just the right addition for an established one, I have chosen over fifty trees, shrubs, climbers and perennial plants for a wide range of positions and uses. The brief descriptions include the plant's common name when it has one, details of its appearance and approximate height and spread. Finally, one or two planting partners are suggested.

Centaurea montana, *known as mountain bluet or perennial cornflower, is very drought-tolerant and easy to grow, being especially at home on an alkaline soil. It is at its best in early summer when the blue flowers will enhance the pink or white of Oriental poppies or be flattered themselves by silvery* Artemisia. *Its long season can be extended still further if it is cut right down as soon as flowering is over because it will shoot again and flower on its secondary growth.*

All the plants listed here will thrive in dry, unimproved soils even without a mulch, although they will do better given such help. Once established, they can tolerate considerable periods of drought in temperate regions. In hot, dry countries some may need thorough watering at intervals during the summer—how frequently will depend on the temperature, humidity and soil type. None of them requires an acid soil, although a few will not thrive in shallow, alkaline soils. Where this is the case, it is mentioned in the description.

The majority of the plants listed are said to be able to withstand temperatures of 5°F (−15°C). The more tender exceptions are indicated. It must be borne in mind, however, that a plant's hardiness is often related to its age and condition, the moisture content of the soil and the duration and frequency of the low temperature, to say nothing of the wind-chill factor.

In making my selection of key plants for the dry garden, the emphasis has been on permanency and multiple attractions, or a long season of interest. This has, regretfully, meant omitting bulbs, annuals and half-hardy plants. However, many of these are described in the chapter "Plants for the dry garden" (see page 53).

Plants in a garden are almost never seen in isolation and their immediate neighbors affect the way in which we view them. Thus, a setting of several plants with small leaves will enhance a single specimen with large leaves, while the character of a narrow, upright conifer will be emphasized by the presence of a low, spreading evergreen. In some positions, this contrast of form may be too stark and we would be better to add to the group a medium-sized shrub of rounded outline. It is the same with color; sometimes the overall scheme calls for complementary colors to be juxtaposed—yellow against purple, or blue with orange. More often we shall want harmony rather than contrast and this goes for texture and foliage color as well as flowers.

In choosing planting partners for these key plants, I have limited myself to the plants described in this chapter so that you may immediately imagine the result and decide to give it a try, or reject it in favor of a combination of your own. I hope in most instances it will be the latter, for finding planting partners and arranging them within the overall pattern of the garden so that the composite is greater than the sum of its parts is one of the most enjoyable challenges that gardening can bring.

Trees

Acer
(Maple)

The large-growing forms of maple are very hardy and will grow in any good well-drained soil. The following are among the best for dry soil.

A. campestre, the field maple, although a medium-sized and round-headed deciduous tree, also makes an excellent hedging plant. The small, five-lobed leaves take on yellow and orange tints in autumn. It is very tolerant of a wide range of soils including alkaline ones. **Size** H and S: 40 ft. **Planting partner** *Cotinus coggygria*.

A. ginnala, the Amur maple, is a small, wide-spreading tree with bright green, three-lobed leaves. Clusters of red-winged fruits appear in autumn and the leaves turn scarlet. **Size** H: 16 ft.; S: 20 ft. **Planting partner** Underplant with *Cotoneaster microphyllus*.

Cercis siliquastrum
(Judas tree)

This bushy, low-forking tree flowers in late spring when the clusters of tiny pea-like blooms, which are anything between rose-pink and rich purple, sprout from the bare twigs and branches in such quantities as to clothe the tree in color. The glaucous blue-green leaves are almost heart-shaped. A sandy soil and plenty of sunshine suit the Judas tree best for, although remarkably hardy, it needs some heat and plenty of sunshine if it is to flower well. In North America, *Cercis canadensis* is an excellent alternative. **Size** H: 13 ft.; S: 23 ft. **Planting partner** *Cistus*.

Cupressus
(Cypress)

Cupressus glabra 'Conica' is a quick-growing, cone-shaped conifer with finely textured, silver-blue foliage which makes an excellent hedge. It can endure heat and drought but is not always long-lived. **Size** H: 33 ft.; S: 25 ft. **Planting partner** *Rosa rugosa*.

C. macrocarpa 'Goldcrest,' the Monterey cypress, is another fast-growing, upright conifer with golden-yellow foliage on red stems. It is unable to survive temperatures below 23°F (−5°C) and will not withstand clipping. It thrives in coastal gardens. **Size** H: 40 ft.; S: 10 ft. **Planting partner** *Juniperus communis repanda*.

Gleditsia triacanthos
(Honey locust)

A large, quick-growing, deciduous tree of rounded habit, up to 70 ft. tall with a spread of 50 ft., the honey locust's frond-like foliage does not unfold until late spring, which makes it a good lawn tree. The cultivars below are a very good choice because they do not have the sharp thorns of the original species.

Planting partners Tall pines make a particularly good backdrop, especially for *Gleditsia* which has green or yellow leaves; *Cupressus glabra* is better for 'Ruby Lace.'

G. triacanthos 'Ruby Lace' has deep red young foliage which changes to bronze. **Size** H: 40 ft.; S: 25 ft.

G. triacanthos 'Sunburst' has rich yellow leaves which change to green. **Size** H: 40 ft.; S: 25 ft.

Golden rain tree
see *Koelreuteria paniculata*

Honey locust
see *Gleditsia triacanthos*

Judas tree see *Cercis siliquastrum*

Juniperus
(Juniper)

Junipers provide some of the best conifers for the dry garden, whether its climate is near-Arctic or subtropical. They thrive in any reasonable soil, including alkaline types. Although preferring sun, they will tolerate some shade, especially in hot countries.

J. communis repanda is among the best junipers for ground cover. The dull green needle-like leaves take on bronze tints in winter.
Size H: 1 ft.; S: 4 ft. **Planting partner** *Genista lydia*.

J. horizontalis 'Wiltonii' has long, spreading branches and develops, in time, into a blue-gray rug.
Size H: 6 in.; S: 8 ft. **Planting partner** *Rosa* 'Dunwich Rose.'

J. × *media* 'Gold Coast' slowly produces a flat-topped specimen with golden-tipped foliage.
Size H: 3 ft.; S: 4 ft. **Planting partner** *Lavandula angustifolia* 'Munstead.'

J. scopulorum 'Skyrocket' makes a blue-gray, pencil-thin column.
Size H: 26 ft.; S: 2½ ft. **Planting partner** *J. horizontalis* 'Wiltonii'.

J. chinensis 'Kaizuka,' the Hollywood juniper, an irregular, spreading bush with long branches clothed in bright green foliage growing out at various angles, is useful as a background to other plants.
Size H: 16 ft.; S: 13 ft. **Planting partner** *Cytisus*.

Koelreuteria paniculata
(Golden rain tree)

This is a small deciduous tree of open habit with long, pinnate leaves which are reddish in spring before turning dark green, and then bright yellow in autumn. The small yellow flowers in upright panicles are produced in late summer and are followed by brown, papery seedpods. This tree is good on sandy soils as long as it has enough sun to ripen the wood.
Size H and S: 33 ft. **Planting partner** Underplant with *Mahonia*.

Maple see *Acer*

Pinus
(Pine)

Most pines like sun, light soils and good drainage but, with a few exceptions, are not adapted to drought when it is combined with high temperatures and drying winds. In any case, most plants grow too large for the average modern garden and their dislike of atmospheric pollution makes them particularly unsuitable for our towns and cities.

P. nigra, the Austrian pine, makes a broadly conical, rather open tree which loses its bottom branches with age. The needles are dark green. Tolerant of exposure, it makes a first-class wind-

Acer ginnala

All gardens, however small, need a tree; it may be as a feature, for shelter, shade, privacy or simply to give a sense of height.

break both inland and on the coast.
Size H: 60 ft.; S: 40 ft. **Planting partner** *Elaeagnus angustifolia*.

P. radiata, the Monterey pine, grows much more rapidly but is not as hardy as other pines. It makes an excellent tree for shelter belts in milder districts and by the ocean. Its needles are long, soft and bright green.
Size H: 60 ft.; S: 30 ft. **Planting partner** *Cistus*.

P. mugo, the mugo pine, is a natural dwarf with a spreading, irregular habit and dark green in color. *P. mugo pumilio* is one of a number of garden pines of smaller size and more even shape.
Size H: 4 ft.; S: 8 ft. **Planting partners** A ground-cover planting of dwarf *Sedum* and thyme.

Shrubs and climbers

Abelia

All the abelias are pretty, if unspectacular, small shrubs which are partially evergreen in mild climates and suitable for sun or light shade. *A. × grandiflora* has pale pink, trumpet-shaped flowers in late summer and autumn, enhanced by reddish bracts which persist after the flowers fade. It will grow on both sand and clay, forms a low hedge and can even be trained on a wall. 'Francis Mason' has subtly variegated leaves of soft yellow and green and needs protection from strong sunlight. *A.* 'Edward Goucher' has darker pink flowers.

Size H: 5 ft.; S: 4 ft. **Planting partner** *Ceratostigma plumbaginoides*.

Arbutus unedo
(Strawberry tree)

Taking many years to reach tree-like stature, this plant is more often seen as a large evergreen shrub. It likes full or dappled sunlight and can withstand

Arbutus unedo

heat and coastal conditions, although it may not survive prolonged exposure to temperatures below 16°F (−9°C). It has dark, glossy leaves on red stalks, rough, fox-red bark, clusters of small, pitcher-shaped, white or pink flowers in autumn, with red fruits at the same time, the product of the previous year's flowers.

Size H: 33 ft.; S: 20 ft. **Planting partner** *Elaeagnus × ebbingei* 'Gilt Edge.'

Brachyglottis

Brachyglottis (syn. *Senecio*) 'Sunshine' has smooth, felted leaves on nearly white stems and yellow daisy-like flowers which open from silver buds in midsummer. Although it will grow in semi-shade, it will be a better color and remain more compact if planted in full sun. A better growth will be achieved if pruning is undertaken as soon as the flowers fade. It is important that you completely cut out all the badly placed stems and shorten the remainder.

Size H: 3 ft.; S: 5 ft. **Planting partner** *Viburnum tinus*.

Broom see *Cytisus*

Buddleia
(Butterfly bush)

Few people would wish to be without a buddleia or two and for the new gardener their rapid growth is a boon. *B. davidii* is an old favorite. Easily struck from cuttings, it grows on any soil and is beloved for the butterflies

that crowd its honey-scented, arching spikes in late summer. Larger flowers can be produced if the bush is hard-pruned in late winter. Its cultivars include 'Black Knight' (violet-purple); 'Pink Pearl'; 'Peace' (white); and 'Harlequin' (red-purple with yellow and green variegated leaves). *B.* 'Lochinch' gains in having soft-gray leaves as a setting for its lavender-blue flowers produced in late summer.

Size H: 6½ ft.; S: 8 ft. **Planting partner** *Romneya coulteri*.

Butterfly bush see *Buddleja*

Californian tree poppy
see *Romneya coulteri*

Californian wild lilac see *Ceanothus*

Ceanothus
(Californian wild lilac)

This genus of both evergreen and deciduous shrubs needs plenty of sunshine, while a free-draining acid or neutral soil suits them best. They hate being subjected to constant irrigation. The evergreen kinds grow rapidly and have numerous tiny flowers which almost hide the foliage. They are unable to withstand temperatures much below 23°F (−5°C) and the upright-growing sorts need a sunny wall. Any pruning to keep them in bounds must be done immediately after flowering. The deciduous varieties are hardier and flower in late summer and, except in very cold gardens, will grow in open positions. As these ceanothus flower on young wood, they should be pruned in spring.

C. 'Cascade' is one of the best cultivars for a high wall as its semi-pendulous branches are more graceful than most. The medium-blue flowers appear just as spring is passing into summer. **Size H and S:** 16 ft. growing on a wall. **Planting partner** *Helianthemum* 'Rhodanthe Carneum.'

C. impressus blooms three weeks earlier than *C.* 'Cascade' and does not get quite as large. Its tiny, corrugated leaves are dark green and the flowers a rich deep blue.
Size H and S: 10 ft. on a wall. **Planting partner** *Choisya ternata.*

C. thyrsiflorus repens grows horizontally, quickly making dense ground cover, instead of making a tall, bushy shrub, or even a small tree. The pale blue flowers are borne in racemes in late spring. It is somewhat hardier than the upright forms.
Size H: 3 ft.; **S:** 8 ft. **Planting partners** *Cistus × skanbergii, Genista lydia.*

C. × delileanus 'Gloire de Versailles' is the best known deciduous kind, with broad, oval, mid-green leaves and powder-blue flowers on its arching branches in summer and autumn. 'Topaz' has deeper-blue flowers.
Size H and S: 6 ft. **Planting partner** *Lavatera* 'Barnsley.'

Ceratostigma
(Plumbago)

Shrubs with blue flowers and shrubs which flower after midsummer are in the minority. *Ceratostigma*, with its small, blue flowers carried well into autumn, scores on both points.

C. willmottianum produces a cluster of thin stems which should be pruned almost to ground level in spring. It will grow in any soil but needs plenty of sun. It is reasonably hardy when established but should be planted in spring and given a mulch. Small, rich blue flowers with paler centers appear in late summer and autumn.
Size H: 2½ ft.; **S:** 2 ft. **Planting partner** *Rosa glauca.*

C. plumbaginoides behaves much more like a herbaceous plant, disappearing in winter. It spreads quite rapidly and makes good ground cover. The flowers are a darker blue and appear in autumn, when the leaves turn red.
Size H: 1 ft.; **S:** 2 ft. **Planting partner** *Lonicera japonica* 'Aureoreticulata.'

Cistus
(Rock rose)

Although these evergreen shrubs can withstand heat, drought, poor alkaline soil and salt spray, they are unable to survive cold winters. Even the hardier ones are unlikely to survive a temperature drop to 18°F (−8°C). Flowers appear in early summer in such quantities that it does not matter that individually they last but a day. They are best suited to the West coast conditions in North America.
Planting partners *Ceanothus thyrsiflorus repens, Ruta graveolens* 'Jackman's Blue.'

C. × cyprius has large white flowers, with a dark red blotch at the base of each petal, and sage-green leaves.
Size H and S: 6 ft.

C. × purpureus has cerise-pink flowers

*Ceratostigma
plumbaginoides*

Shrubs are the essential component of every garden, providing a permanent framework of woody stems which are clothed in attractive foliage and, in most cases, beautiful flowers and/or fruit in due season.

with a chocolate-colored center. Its narrow leaves are strongly aromatic.
Size H: 5 ft.; **S:** 6 ft.

C. × skanbergii has narrow, gray-green leaves, which combine well with the small, clear pink flowers.
Size H: 3 ft.; **S:** 4 ft.

C. × corbariensis (syn. *C. × hybridus*) is among the hardiest of the rock roses with dark green, wavy-edged leaves. The flowering season is shorter than most, the red buds opening to small white flowers with a yellow center.
Size H: 3 ft.; **S:** 4 ft.

Cotoneaster lacteus

Cotoneaster

Cotoneasters grow well on dry soils but prefer them to contain humus. They should not be left for months without water but they do make good coastal shrubs.

C. lacteus is an evergreen shrub with arching branches clothed in leathery leaves which are dark green above and gray beneath. Although the creamy white flowers are not particularly eye-catching, the clusters of small red berries ripen late and are retained until spring. It is excellent as an informal hedge and for training on shady walls. **Size** H and S: 10 ft. **Planting partner** *Elaeagnus × ebbingei* 'Gilt Edge.'

C. microphyllus is also evergreen with prostrate main branches and arching laterals. It has tiny, dark green leaves and small white flowers, much favored by bees, and rose-red berries. **Size** H: 2½ ft.; S: 6 ft. **Planting partner** *Genista lydia*.

Cotton lavender see *Santolina*

Culinary sage see *Salvia officinalis*

Cytisus
(Broom)

The clustered stems of most brooms are such a bright green that although deciduous they make an impact even in winter. The flowers, unlike the very small leaves, are showy and come in late spring or early summer. Brooms need full sun and a soil which is not too limy. Shear them several times in their first season and trim annually after flowering to prevent them from becoming leggy and unattractive.

C. × praecox has masses of creamy-yellow flowers from mid- to late spring. There is a white form, 'Albus,' and the bright yellow 'Goldspeer.' **Size** H and S: 5 ft. **Planting partners** *Cotoneaster microphyllus, Erica*.

C. scoparius, the Scotch broom, has many cultivars ranging from yellow and orange to crimson and lilac-pink. There are also many bicolors. The old, tall-growing 'Cornish Cream' is still one of the best. Among the newer introductions is the excellent, bushy 'Lena' which is orange-red. All flower in late spring or early summer. **Size** H and S: 5 ft. **Planting partners** *Brachyglottis* 'Sunshine' and rosemary (*Rosmarinus*).

C. battandieri, the Moroccan broom, is often not recognized as a broom by people seeing it for the first time. Its brown stems are sparsely covered in silky, silvery leaves and the stubby flowers, produced in early summer, are shaped like miniature corn cobs and scented like pineapples. Not completely hardy, in very cold districts it needs only the shelter of a sunny wall. **Size** H: 10 ft.; S: 6 ft. **Planting partners** *Iris germanica* and *Rosa* 'Blanche Double de Coubert.'

Elaeagnus

These large-growing shrubs can tolerate wind, salt and shade. Their foliage is coated with silvery scales and they produce insignificant but strongly scented flowers followed, in some cases, by attractive fruit.

Cotinus
(Smoke bush)

The multiplicity of flower stalks which remain after the insignificant flowers have faded in late summer look like puffs of pink smoke, fading to gray.

C. coggygria is deciduous, its rounded, slightly glaucous leaves turning yellow or orange in autumn. **Size** H: 10 ft.; S: 8 ft. **Planting partner** *Ceanothus* 'Gloire de Versailles.'

C. coggygria 'Royal Purple' has deep, purple-brown leaves. The "smoke" is much less obvious. **Size** H: 6 ft.; S: 5 ft. **Planting partners** *Abelia × grandiflora, Artemisia stelleriana, Perovskia* 'Blue Spire.'

E. angustifolia, oleaster or the Russian olive, makes a spiny, tree-like specimen with silvery-gray willow-like leaves. Its flowers, which come in spring, are followed by small yellow, olive-like fruits with silver scales.
Size H: 20 ft.; S: 10 ft. **Planting partner** *Cotoneaster lacteus*.

E. × ebbingei 'Gilt Edge' is among the best variegated evergreen shrubs, showing little inclination to revert to plain green. The polished leaves are margined with yellow.
Size H: 6 ft.; S: 5 ft. **Planting partner** *Cotoneaster microphyllus*.

Escallonia

This genus of quick-growing, semi- or completely evergreen shrubs has small, chalice-shaped flowers in shades of pink, white and red which are produced freely in early summer and intermittently into autumn. They are ideal for windswept coastal gardens and prefer alkaline or sandy soils. Tolerant of clipping, they make excellent hedges. They vary somewhat in hardiness, the small-leaved sorts being tougher in general. None will withstand temperatures much lower than 16°F without damage and is largely restricted to West Coast areas.
Planting partners *Artemisia* 'Powis Castle' and *Ruta graveolens* 'Jackman's Blue.'

E. rubra 'Crimson Spire,' with comparatively large, glossy, dark green leaves, is excellent for hedging.
Size H: 10 ft.; S: 6 ft.

E. 'Donard Seedling' has small leaves and semi-pendulous branches. The flesh-pink buds open to white blooms

flushed with pale rose-pink.
Size H: 8 ft.; S: 6 ft.

E. 'Donard Star', although less hardy, has beautiful rose-pink flowers.
Size H and S: 5 ft.

Genista

A close relative of the broom *(Cytisus)* and with similar green stems and small leaves, *Genista* has the advantage of being able to grow on alkaline soil.

G. aetnensis, the Mount Etna broom, is a sparsely branched yet graceful, tree-like shrub. In late summer, masses of tiny, clear yellow flowers crowd the endmost twigs.
Size H: 15 ft.; S: 10 ft. **Planting partner** Lavender *(Lavandula)*.

G. lydia has thin, arching twigs and strong yellow flowers in early summer.
Size H: 2 ft.; S: 3 ft. **Planting partner** *Salvia officinalis* 'Purpurascens.'

G. pilosa 'Vancouver Gold' is completely prostrate and excellent as ground cover, for draping over rocks and over the face of a retaining wall. The yellow flowers come in late spring.
Size H: 6 in.; S: 4 ft. **Planting partner** *Helianthemum* 'The Bride.'

Hedera
(Ivy)

Ivy is valuable as a covering for shady walls, as a carpet under trees or around the base of large shrubs where few other plants will grow. In addition, its deep roots and dense growth are excellent for preventing soil erosion. Two of the best ivies, both with large, heart-shaped leaves, are the slightly tender

H. algeriensis 'Gloire de Marengo' (syn. *H. canariensis* 'Variegata'), beautifully marbled in green and gray and edged with white, and *H. colchica* 'Sulfur Heart,' which is hardier. *H. helix*, or the common English ivy, has smaller, lobed leaves in the traditional ivy shape. 'Glacier' has small gray leaves edged with white; 'Goldheart' is green with a bold yellow flash which is less suitable as a ground-cover plant.
Size H: At least 10 ft.; S: over 12 ft. **Planting partners** *Iris foetidissima* for ground cover; *Lonicera japonica* 'Halliana' for climbers.

Cytisus battandieri

Ivy see *Hedera*

Japanese honeysuckle
see *Lonicera japonica*

Lavandula

(Lavender)

Lavender is so well known that a description is superfluous—even the scent can be identified by most people. It needs a free-draining soil and full sun. The faded flower spikes are best removed in autumn and the bushes trimmed in spring.

L. angustifolia 'Munstead' has dark lavender-blue flowers which are produced in mid- to late summer.

Lavatera 'Barnsley'

Size H: 1½ ft.; 2 ft. **Planting**

partner *Romneya coulteri*.

L. angustifolia 'Hidcote' has deep purple flowers which open a little later.
Size H: 1½ ft.; S: 1½ ft. **Planting partner** *Brachyglottis* 'Sunshine.'

L. vera, Dutch lavender, has the best silvery foliage. The long flower spikes are a soft gray-blue and appear in late summer or early autumn.
Size H: 2½ ft.; S: 3 ft. **Planting partner** *Rosa rugosa* 'Fru Dagmar Hastrup.'

L. stoechas, French lavender, bears purple-blue flowers in early summer topped by a tuft of purple bracts.
Size H: 2 ft.; S: 1½ ft. **Planting partner** *Helianthemum*.

Lavatera

(Tree mallow)

These fast-growing, soft, semi-evergreen shrubs are usually treated more like herbaceous plants and pruned almost to the ground in spring. They are not completely hardy and survive best on dry soils and by the sea. *L. olbia* 'Rosea' has hairy, lobed leaves and rose-pink, hollyhock-like flowers which are produced ceaselessly from midsummer to early autumn. *L.* 'Barnsley' has very pale pink flowers with a dark crimson center.
Size H and S: 6 ft. **Planting partner** *Perovskia* 'Blue Spire.'

Lonicera japonica

(Japanese honeysuckle)

This species of honeysuckle can adapt to drought conditions once established. Deciduous or evergreen de-

pending on the severity of the climate, it flowers from midsummer to autumn in sun or shade, with the flowers appearing in the leaf axils, and is strongly perfumed both by day and night. When grown on a wall, it needs support. It can also be used as ground cover, but may need restraining because it can take root as it spreads. Always cut it hard back in spring to prevent an accumulation of dead wood. 'Halliana' has pale green leaves and white flowers turning to buff as they age. 'Aureoreticulata' has green leaves netted with bright yellow veins and sparse but strongly scented white flowers. The young leaves of *L. japonica repens* are reddish-purple and the white flowers open from red buds.
Size H: 15 ft.; S: 10 ft. **Planting partner** *Ceanothus impressus*.

Mahonia

These handsome evergreen shrubs prefer moist, well-drained soil but they will withstand considerable drought, given shade and shelter.

M. japonica has long, pinnate, spiny leaves, which are glossy and dark green. Tiny, lily-of-the-valley-scented bell flowers are borne in winter, followed by blue-black berries.
Size H and S: 6 ft. **Planting partner** *Hedera helix* 'Glacier' as a ground cover.

M. pinnata makes a dense bush with shiny, dark green, wavy-edged leaves and heads of densely packed yellow flowers in early spring.
Size H: 5 ft.; S: 4 ft. **Planting partner** *Iris foetidissima* 'Variegata.'

Perovskia
(Russian sage)

Perovskia atriplicifolia has finely cut, gray-green foliage and white stems which carry clusters of lavender-blue flowers from late summer into autumn. Both leaves and stems have a sage-like aroma if bruised. It needs a well-drained soil and an open position as it will sprawl unless given full sun. In spring, it should be cut almost to the ground to obtain strong growth and better flowers. 'Blue Spire' has flowers of a richer color.
Size H: 4 ft.; S: 4 ft. **Planting partner** *Buddleja*.

Plumbago see *Ceratostigma*

Rock rose see *Cistus*

Romneya coulteri
syn. *R.* × *hybrida*
(Californian tree poppy)

This is really a subshrub which becomes woody and shrub-like when winters are mild but dies back to the ground if subjected to frosts. It has glaucous leaves and stems bearing big, white, poppy-like flowers in late summer which have crinkled petals and prominent golden stamens. It needs sun and has no objection to a sandy or stony soil. If planted on a rich soil or given irrigation, it will colonize a considerable area, its roots invading those of other plants. To survive temperatures below 23°F (−5°C) it must be given a mulch of bracken fern or bark.
Size H: 5 ft.; S: 4 ft. **Planting partner** *Buddleia* 'Lochinch.'

Rosa
(Rose)

Although most roses manage to survive in uncongenial soils and situations and still provide a few flowers, only a few, such as the ones described below, are actually happy on dry soils.

R. rugosa thrives on sandy as well as other soil types and will grow right down to the edge of the sea. The stems are covered with prickles, while the dark green, deeply veined leaves often change to clear yellow in autumn. Unlike most roses, it makes a dense, shapely bush, is remarkably free of disease and is untroubled by the usual rose pests. In gardens it is usual to plant cultivars which have been developed by crossing *R. rugosa* with other kinds of rose. Three which resemble their wild ancestors are 'Blanche Double de Coubert' with semi-double white flowers and a few hips; 'Roseraie de l'Hay' which has richly scented, double crimson flowers; and 'Fru Dagmar Hastrup' whose clear, light pink flowers are followed by hips the size and color of cherry tomatoes. All the *rugosa* roses flower from early summer for about four months.
Size H: 5 ft.; S: 6 ft. **Planting partner** Purple, lavender or white *Iris germanica*.

R. pimpinellifolia, the wild burnet or Scots briar, colonizes sand dunes with its suckers. It has fern-like leaves and small, single white flowers produced in profusion just as spring gives way to summer. The best forms include 'Dunwich Rose' which is only 2 ft. tall with single, pale yellow flowers; 'Harisonii' (syn. *R.* × *harisonii* 'Harison's Yellow'), a taller, semi-double, bril-

Romneya coulteri

liant yellow cultivar; 'Stanwell Perpetual', so called because it continues to produce its scented, double, blush-pink blooms well into the autumn; and 'William III,' a low bush with semi-double, purple flowers.
Size H and S: 3 ft. **Planting partner** *Nepeta*.

R. glauca (syn. *R. rubrifolia*) can adapt to dry soils and take more shade than most roses. Both stems and leaves are wine-red with a gray sheen. The single pink flowers produced in early summer are succeeded by clusters of oval-shaped red hips.
Size H and S: 6 ft. **Planting partners** *Artemisia* 'Lambrook Silver,' *Centranthus ruber coccineus*.

Santolina
chamaecyparissus
and S. pinnata

Rosmarinus officinalis
(Rosemary)

Rosemary is as indispensable in the garden as it is in the kitchen. The narrow evergreen leaves are medium-green on the upper surface and almost white beneath and, as they are held vertically, the bush appears gray at a little distance. The pale blue flowers are produced over a long period starting in early spring. It needs full sun and a poor dry soil, so do not fertilize or irrigate. If the natural, sprawling growth is not to your taste, prune after flowering, or plant the cultivar 'Miss Jessopp's Upright,' although the color is only a milky blue.

Size H: 5 ft.; S: 6 ft. **Planting partner** *Euphorbia characias wulfenii*.

Rue see *Ruta graveolens*

Russian sage see *Perovskia*

Ruta graveolens
'Jackman's Blue'
(Rue)

This compact little bush has delicate, finely cut leaves in a striking shade of steel-blue, an almost unique color. The clusters of yellow flowers are of no great attraction but only a few will be produced if the plant is cut back every spring to keep it tidy and encourage the best foliage. Rue has two drawbacks: it has an unpleasant smell if bruised and, more seriously, can raise blisters on the skin for those allergic to it. Always take precautions when working with or near rue.

Size H: 2 ft.; S: 3 ft. **Planting partners** *Euphorbia characias wulfenii*, *Salvia* 'Icterina.'

Salvia officinalis
(Culinary sage)

The purple-leaved form of culinary sage is known as *S. officinalis* 'Purpurascens' and is just as useful in the kitchen. Its soft young shoots and new leaves, which gradually fade to gray, are delightful, especially when combined with its spikes of violet flowers in early summer. *S. officinalis* 'Tricolor' mixes cream, red and gray in its leaves and 'Icterina' mixes gray and yellow. These do not flower and are less hardy than the purple kind.

Size H: 2 ft.; S: 3 ft. **Planting partners** *Artemisia*, *Helianthemum* and *Ruta*.

Santolina
(Cotton lavender)

In spite of its common name, this shrub bears no relation to either cotton or lavender, being a member of the Compositae or daisy family—not that its flowers, which appear in late summer, look much like daisies either, being button-shaped and lacking in petals! All types of *Santolina* make small, dome-shaped shrubs with soft, feathery, aromatic foliage. They are reasonably hardy on all soils but survive best on dry, infertile ones and in full sun. Pruning the stems back to the woody stump every spring is necessary to keep growth compact.

Planting partner *Cotinus coggygria* 'Royal Purple.'

S. chamaecyparissus (syn. *S. incana*) looks as if it is covered with hoarfrost and has harsh yellow flowers.

Size H: 1½ ft.; S: 2 ft.

S. pinnata (syn. *S. neapolitana*) is larger than the above species with more feathery leaves and its flowers are a more pleasant shade of pale yellow.

Size H: 2½ ft.; S: 3 ft.

S. rosmarinifolia (syn. *S. virens*) has rich green leaves and strong yellow flowers. The cultivar 'Primrose Gem' is a more attractive shade of yellow.

Size H: 1½ ft.; S: 2 ft.

Senecio cineraria
syn. *S. maritimus*

Senecio cineraria, or dusty miller, is a gray-leaved, evergreen shrub which thrives in coastal locations. The cultivar 'Silver Dust' is usually grown from seed as an annual for summer bedding, although plants will often survive a winter or two. Far better and more permanent, provided they are given a warm soil and sun, are the cultivars 'Ramparts,' which has deeply lobed leaves, and 'White Diamond' with chrysanthemum-like leaves which overlap to create a solid white dome. All produce "ragwort"-type daisies in late summer unless the plants are hard pruned in spring.

Size H: 1½ ft.; S: 2 ft. **Planting partner** *Cotinus coggygria* 'Royal Purple.'

Smoke bush see *Cotinus*

Spanish broom
see *Spartium junceum*

Spartium junceum
(Spanish broom)

A fast-growing, almost leafless shrub with sprays of large, sweetly scented, yellow pea-like flowers which appear on green stems from midsummer until autumn. By nature upright, leggy and of open habit, it can be kept shorter and induced to grow more densely by removing all but an inch or so of the previous year's growth each spring. When subjected to plenty of sun, wind and a dry sandy soil, as by the sea, this treatment is unlikely to be necessary. **Size** H: 9 ft.; S: 7 ft. **Planting partner** *Buddleia* 'Black Knight.'

Strawberry tree see *Arbutus unedo*

Tree mallow see *Lavatera*

Viburnum tinus

Most viburnums need a moist soil but this well-known shrub can withstand both drought and heat given a reasonably fertile soil. It makes an excellent screen or hedge, although its growth is slow for the first few years. It can grow in shade and is often placed under trees as a result, but it will flower and produce attractive, blue-black fruit in late summer more freely given some sun. The dark evergreen leaves show up the flat heads of tiny white flowers in winter and early spring. The best forms are 'Gwenllian' with its pink-tinged flowers and 'Eve Price' which is more compact and has carmine-shaded flowers. 'Bewley's Variegated' has green, gold and gray leaves which combine well with the pink flowers. **Size** H and S: 10 ft. **Planting partner** *Hedera algeriensis* 'Gloire de Marengo' as ground cover.

Yucca

With their tough sword-like leaves arranged in rosettes, these extraordinary evergreens can bring a touch of the desert even to a cold garden. The white or cream flowers are waxy, bell-shaped and held in long panicles high above the leaves from midsummer to autumn, depending on the species. All yuccas do best in full sun and on warm light soil, but they will grow in semi-shade and on heavier, colder soils. **Planting partners** *Achillea tomentosa*, *Stachys byzantina* 'Silver Carpet.'

Y. filamentosa, or Adam's needle, has tufts of dark green leaves edged with curling white threads. 'Bright Edge' is a good variegated form. *Y. flaccida* 'Golden Sword' is also variegated but more golden, and less free-flowering. **Size** H: 2½ ft.; S: 3 ft.

Y. gloriosa, unlike *Y. filamentosa* and the similar *Y. flaccida*, which are stemless with their leaves rising directly from the ground, slowly develops a thick trunk crowned with a rosette of sword-shaped leaves which have sharp tips. The flower panicles rise to a height of 6½ ft. on established plants. The variegated form is striking but it flowers later. **Size** H: 5 ft.; S: 4 ft.

Yucca gloriosa

Perennials

Acanthus
(Bear's breeches)

Handsome and long-lived, bear's breeches produce mounds of large, deeply cut leaves in spring, above which, in midsummer, rise stems ringed with mauve and white flowers beneath slightly sinister, purple-hooded bracts which end in sharp prickles. These plants prefer sun in cool countries, shade in hot ones. They thrive in any garden soil and have very long roots which are difficult to eradicate once they are established, so their position in the garden needs to be chosen with care. Due to their distinctive foliage, they should not be screened by other plants.

Planting partners *Achillea tomentosa* and *Stachys* in front of *Rosa glauca*.

A. mollis latifolius has the largest leaves which are soft, waxy and rather lax.

Size H: 5 ft.; S: 3 ft.

A. spinosus has darker, glossier and more finely cut leaves, and produces flowers with greater freedom.

Size H: 4 ft.; S: 2 ft

Achillea
(Yarrow)

With fern-like leaves and flat heads of tightly clustered, daisy-like flowers, yarrow is a mainstay of classic herbaceous borders. They flower freely throughout the summer, especially in the sun, but need frequent division because they spread so rapidly. They are good for cutting and the tall sorts can be dried for winter decorations.

A. 'Moonshine' is silvery leaved with clear, pale yellow flowers.

Size H: 2 ft.; S: 1½ ft. **Planting partner** *Coreopsis verticillata* 'Golden Shower.'

A. 'Coronation Gold' has gray-green leaves and bright yellow, plate-like flowers.

Size H: 3 ft.; S: 2 ft. **Planting partner** *Salvia × superba*.

A. tomentosa is one of several ground-hugging types, forming a mat of dark green leaves with cream flowers. It is evergreen in mild climates where it can be kept compact by clipping almost to the ground in spring.

Size H: 6 in; S: 1½ ft. **Planting partner** *Helianthemum*.

Anthemis

These are perennials which need full sun and a well-drained soil—on soils which lie wet in winter they are inclined to be short-lived. Until recently, botanists included chamomile in this family of plants and, indeed, most of the species have some of the same scent in their leaves.

A. punctata cupaniana makes a ground-covering carpet of dense, finely divided, silvery foliage which turns green in winter. Large, daisy-like flowers with a yellow center and pure white petals cover the plant in late spring or early summer.

Size H: 1 ft.; S: 2 ft. **Planting partner** *Cistus × purpureus*.

A. tinctoria is of shrubby growth with feathery, medium-green leaves and masses of 2 in. wide yellow daisies from mid- to late summer. Plants are inclined to sprawl unless they are supported with twigs. There are numerous cultivars with colors ranging from deep yellow as in 'Grallach Gold,' to cream as in 'Wargrave.'

Size H: 2½ ft.; S: 2 ft. **Planting partners** *Salvia nemorosa*, *Lonicera nitida* 'Baggesen's Gold.'

Artemisia

This genus contains some of the very best silver foliage plants available with mostly inconspicuous flowers. They are reasonably hardy but need full sun and a well-drained soil—they cannot stand being waterlogged in winter. Sparrows sometimes strip the young foliage; if this happens, protect the plants with black cotton or wire pea netting until the shoots harden.

Anthemis punctata cupaniana

Planting partners *Rosa glauca* and *Salvia officinalis* 'Purpurascens.'
A. absinthium 'Lambrook Silver' has a woody base from which shoot silky, much-divided leaves. The flowers, which appear in late summer, are tiny yellow bobbles on long spikes and should be cut back as they fade.
Size H and S: 2 ft.
A. alba 'Canescens' has needle-thin, curling leaves on woody stems which sprawl before turning upward. It should be planted in groups or drifts for the best effect.
Size H and S: 1½ ft.
A. 'Powis Castle' is like a shrubby 'Lambrook Silver' but its woody stems should be pruned nearly to the base in spring to keep the bush solid.
Size H: 2½ ft.; S: 3 ft.
A. stelleriana has leaves which, although deeply lobed, are substantial and a silvery white. The plant makes a sprawling mound.
Size H: 1 ft.; S: 2 ft.

Bear's breeches see *Acanthus*

Cardoon see *Cynara cardunculus*

Catmint see *Nepeta*

Centaurea
(Knapweed)

A family of sun-loving, easy-to-grow plants which includes those attractive annuals cornflower *(C. cyanus)* and sweet sultan *(C. moschata)* as well as the perennials described below. Typically they have long, narrow-lobed leaves and hard globular buds covered with papery scales from which thin tubular fringed petals emerge around a thistle-like center.
C. cineraria cineraria is a beautiful, almost shrubby, foliage plant with rosettes of 1 ft. long lacy leaves coated in silvery velvet which droop so as to hide the stems. The small purple flowers come in late summer but are almost hidden in the foliage. Unfortunately, it will only withstand a few degrees of frost but is more likely to survive on a very dry, poor soil. Soft cuttings taken in late summer and over-wintered in a cold frame are an insurance against losses.
Size H: 2 ft.; S: 1½ ft. **Planting partner** *Sedum* 'Ruby Glow.'
C. hypoleuca 'John Coutts' forms spreading clumps of dissected leaves, soft green above and gray beneath. Deep pink flowers with a pale yellow center are produced over a long period in summer. It makes an excellent ground-cover plant.
Size H and S: 1½ ft. **Planting partners** *Rosa* 'Roseraie de l'Hay,' *Artemisia* 'Lambrook Silver.'
C. macrocephala makes a strong clump of deeply cut, medium-green leaves which, in early summer, throws up rigid stems topped with big, brown, scaly buds. These then open to a mass of golden yellow florets.
Size H: 3 ft.; S: 2 ft. **Planting partner** *Centranthus ruber albus.*
C. montana is useful in that it flowers freely in late spring and into summer, particularly if dead-headed. The large, cornflower heads on rather sprawling stems are typically blue although there are pink and white forms. The leaves

Acanthus spinosus

Herbaceous plants add color and sparkle to the garden. Most of those which follow have been chosen for their flowers, but others are included for their outstandingly beautiful foliage or dramatic form.

are gray and hairy. On heavy soil it tends to spread rapidly and may be difficult to control as every root left in the soil will make a new plant.
Size H and S: 1½ ft. **Planting partner** *Anthemis tinctoria.*
C. ruthenica makes a clump of attractive, dark green, finely cut leaves above which fluffy, creamy yellow thistle-like flowers are displayed on slender, branched stems in early summer.
Size H: 4 ft.; S: 1½ ft. **Planting partner** *Salvia × sylvestris* 'Mainacht.'

Helianthemum nummularium

Centranthus ruber
(Pink valerian)

The rose-red form of the pink valerian, which grows wild on rocky coasts, where it pushes tenacious roots into crevices, is *C. ruber coccineus*. Its panicles of tiny flowers open over many weeks in high · summer. *C. ruber* 'Albus' is an equally attractive white form. Both self-seed too freely unless the faded flowers are removed quickly. **Size** H and S: 2½ ft. **Planting partner** *Nepeta*.

Coreopsis verticillata

This neat, upright-growing herbaceous plant requires no staking. Its needle-thin leaves are bespangled with small, yellow, star-shaped flowers for weeks in summer. As an added bonus, the cut flowers last well in water. 'Moonbeam' has pale lemon flowers and 'Golden Shower' has bright yellow flowers on 3 ft. stems. **Size** H: 2½ ft; S: 1 ft. **Planting partner** *Salvia nemorosa* 'Ostfriesland' ('East Friesland').

Cynara cardunculus
(Cardoon)

In the vegetable garden, this root crop can be forced, rather like chicory *(Chichorium)*. It is worth bringing into the flower garden for its huge, deeply cut, silvery leaves and late-summer flowers which resemble deep blue thistles on 6 ft. stems. It is hardy once established but it should be planted in spring and mulched for the first winter or so. To keep the foliage in good condition it is necessary to water occasionally in prolonged droughts. **Size** H: 3 ft.; S: 5 ft. **Planting partner** *Artemisia* 'Powis Castle', *Rosa glauca*.

Euphorbia
(Spurge)

Increasingly popular and with good reason because they are easy to grow in sun or semi-shade, euphorbias are distinct in habit and foliage and flower over a long period. They form a large genus, including the Christmas poinsettia *(E. pulcherrima)*. Although some are quite unsuitable for dry gardens, the following semi-succulents are among the best. One word of warning —the stems are full of a milky sap which can cause irritation to the skin. *E. characias wulfenii* has upright stems clothed in narrow glaucous leaves which make a striking feature. As the old flower stems die, a new generation is already shooting from the base. The flowers are lime-green, or yellow in 'Lambrook Gold,' and arranged in round heads at the top of the stems. They begin to open in early spring and last for many months.

Size H: 4 ft.; S: 3 ft. **Planting partner** *Ruta graveolens* 'Jackman's Blue' or *Santolina*.

E. myrsinites consists of spreading stems which radiate from a central crown. The leaves are fleshy and glaucous, and the yellow-green flowers appear in early spring. It is excellent for planting at the top of a retaining wall or to spill on to paving. **Size** H: 6 in.; S: 2 ft. **Planting partner** *Iris unguicularis*.

E. polychroma brings another splash of golden yellow to the garden just as the daffodils *(Narcissus)* and forsythias are fading but, unlike many spring-flowering plants, it will look attractive until autumn when the foliage often takes on orange tints before dying. **Size** H and S: 1½ ft. **Planting partner** *Centaurea montana*.

Evening primrose see **Oenothera**

Helianthemum
(Sun rose)

For a solid splash of color at the beginning of the summer, combined with low, evergreen ground cover, there is nothing to rival *H. nummularium*. The sprawling habit of the little shrublets is particularly useful for softening the edges of paving. Tolerant of both sandy and clay soils as long as they are well drained, they need full sun. The tiny flowers, which can be double or single, come in white, pink, crimson, orange and yellow; there are even a few bicolors. Leaves can be green or gray. Among the single-color forms are 'Fire Dragon' (scarlet) and

'Jubilee' (double yellow). 'Rhodanthe Carneum,' 'Wisley Primrose,' 'The Bride' (cream) and 'Henfield Brilliant' (orange) have gray foliage. Sun roses are best trimmed after flowering, following which they may have a small second flush of flowers.

Size H: 6 in.; S: 1½ ft. **Planting partners** *Artemisia alba* 'Canescens' and *Salvia × sylvestris* 'Mainacht' ('May Night').

Helictrotrichon sempervirens

There are many good ornamental grasses for the dry garden but I have limited myself to just one, which needs a sunny position. It makes clumps of silver-blue blades from which, in early summer, flower shoots grow to 3 ft. These arch gracefully under the weight of straw-colored flowers. In spring, any dead stems and leaves should be "combed out."

Size H and S: 1 ft. **Planting partner** *Salvia officinalis* 'Icterina' or gray-leaved *Helianthemum*.

Iris

The flowers of iris are a unique shape and very beautiful, and several find their natural home in the dry garden. *I. germanica*, the well-known bearded iris, has clumps of sword-shaped leaves springing from creeping rhizomes that rest on the surface of the soil. The complex flowers, produced in early summer, consist of three erect segments, known as "standards," and three drooping ones, called "falls," on which grow the "beards" composed of

tufts of hair. There are literally hundreds of cultivars in almost every color and combination of colors. They need sun, not only on their foliage but on the rhizome too. When planting, remember not to bury the rhizome and to plant iris about 1 ft. apart.

Size H: 2–4 ft.; S: 1 ft. **Planting partners** *Helianthemum*, *Papaver orientale*.

I. pumila looks like a dwarf bearded iris but flowers in late spring and, again, there are numerous named cultivars. One of the best is the clear medium-blue 'Blue Denim.'

Size H: 6 in.; S: 9 in. **Planting partner** *Cytisus × praecox*.

I. foetidissima citrina, the gladwin iris, is invaluable for growing in dry shade. Its small, delicately veined, soft yellow flowers, produced in early summer, are rather hidden in the foliage but they are succeeded by big, drooping seed-pods which split to reveal rows of bright orange seeds. Even without this autumn display, the leaves alone would qualify this plant for inclusion—they are bright, glossy green and look their best in midwinter.

Size H: 2 ft.; S: 1½ ft. **Planting partner** *Choisya ternata*.

I. foetidissima 'Variegata,' the variegated form of the gladwin iris, has cream-striped leaves. Although barren and not as strong-growing, it is nevertheless welcome.

Size H: 2 ft.; S: 1½ ft. **Planting partner** *Viburnum tinus*.

I. unguicularis is indispensable because it flowers for weeks from mid-winter to early spring. It needs a hot spot against a wall. The leaves are long and rather untidy but this is a small price

to pay for the delicately veined flowers of medium-blue or purple in the cultivar 'Mary Barnard,' and ice-blue in 'Walter Butt.'

Size H: 1 ft.; S: 15 in. **Planting partner** *Thymus × citriodorus* 'Golden King.'

Knapweed see *Centaurea*

Lamb's ears see *Stachys byzantina*

Limonium platyphyllum
syn. *L. latifolium*
(Sea lavender)

This plant tolerates heat and cold but does best on a soil that is not too rich. In late summer large panicles of tiny, lavender-colored flowers on wiry stems almost hide the clumps of large, leathery leaves. The flowerheads can be dried for winter arrangements.

Size H and S: 1½ ft. **Planting partner** *Sedum* 'Ruby Glow.'

Iris foetidissima

Papaver orientale

Nepeta
(Catmint)

Nepeta is the classic plant for softening the edges of borders. It gained its common name because cats love the scent of the foliage and may flatten the loose mounds unless deterred by a few spikes of holly or other prickly leaves. *N. × faassenii* is a sun lover of semi-prostrate habit with woolly, gray-green leaves and spikes of lavender flowers in early summer. If cut back as the flowers fade, there is usually a second flush of them. The dead foliage should not be cut until spring to protect the crown from frost.

Size H: 1 ft.; S: 1½ ft. **Planting partner** *Rosa pimpinellifolia* 'Stanwell Perpetual.'

N. 'Six Hills Giant' blooms at the same time but has richer-colored flowers and larger leaves. It is also tougher and a better choice for clay soils which are wet in winter.

Size H and S: 2½ ft. **Planting partner** *Achillea* 'Coronation Gold.'

Oenothera
(Evening primrose)

The evening primrose family has gained its name because many of its members have yellow, tubular flowers which open as the light begins to fade. Others are day-blooming and in the United States are known as sundrops. **Planting partner** *Salvia nemorosa* 'Ostfriesland' ('East Friesland').

O. missouriensis is prostrate with stout, crimson stems set with long narrow leaves. The large, bright yellow, bell-shaped flowers are carried for several weeks in midsummer. They open in the evening and last 24 hours.

Size H: 9 in.; S: 2 ft.

O. fruticosa 'Fyrverkeri' ('Fireworks'), syn. *O. tetragona* 'Fireworks,' is a sundrop, closing its flowers at night. It makes a basal rosette of narrow foliage and from mid- to late summer produces red stems covered with red buds which open to fragrant, cup-shaped, yellow flowers.

Size H: 15 in.; S: 1 ft.

Oriental poppy
see *Papaver orientale*

Papaver orientale
(Oriental poppy)

The flamboyant flowers of the Oriental poppy are among the largest produced by hardy perennials, sometimes reaching 6 in. across. As a result, the unbranched stems require support. The leaves are lance-shaped, toothed and hairy and die away after the plant has flowered, starting into growth again with the arrival of cooler,

autumn weather. Growth is rapid in spring and flowers are produced in early summer. Numerous cultivars include 'Picotée' (white with pinkish edges to the petals), 'Mrs Perry' (salmon-pink) and 'Perry's White.'

Size H: 3 ft.; S: 2 ft. **Planting partner** *Salvia × sylvestris* 'Mainacht' ('May Night').

Pink valerian see *Centranthus ruber*

Sage see *Salvia*

Salvia
(Sage)

In addition to the shrubby sages, there are useful perennial sages. The easy-to-grow *S. nemorosa* has violet-blue flowers enclosed in reddish-purple bracts on massed spikes over deeply veined leaves. They are effective for a long period in summer. The cultivar 'Ostfriesland' is similar but shorter (1½ ft. tall), and the flowers of the similar-sized *S. × sylvestris* 'Mainacht' are nearer a dark blue.

Size H: 2 ft.; S: 1–1½ ft. **Planting partners** *Achillea*, *Artemisia* 'Lambrook Silver.'

Sea lavender
see *Limonium platyphyllum*

Sedum
(Stonecrop)

This genus includes plants which are suitable for rock or scree gardens, others of rapidly spreading growth which make good ground cover and taller kinds for borders.

Planting partner *Helictrotrichon sempervirens, Perovskia* 'Blue Spire.'

S. acre is a mat-forming Alpine, with pale green leaves and tiny, yellow, summer flowers, that roots as it spreads. It will grow on tiled or thatched roofs. On the ground it can spread too much but is easy to pull up. The golden-leaved form, *aureum*, is especially bright in spring.

Size H: 2 in.; S: 1 ft.

S. spathulifolium is a carpeting rock plant made up of tiny rosettes of plump, gray leaves which turn red as they age. Little yellow flowers open from pink buds in early summer.

Size H: 2 in.; S: 1 ft.

S. spectabile 'Brilliant', the iceplant, has flat flowerheads made up of hundreds of tiny, star-shaped, mauve-pink flowers which attract bees and butterflies in early autumn. The glaucous, gray-green leaves are beautiful from spring onward and even in winter the withered flowerheads and leafless brown stems, still attached to the fleshy rosettes at ground level, are not without attraction.

Size H and S: 15 in.

S. 'Herbstfreude' ('Autumn Joy') resembles a larger and stronger edition of *S. spectabile* and shares all its good qualities. The flowers start salmon-pink on opening in early autumn but gradually turn copper-red.

Size H and S: 2 ft.

S. 'Ruby Glow' has heads of dusky red flowers, from late summer to early autumn, on arching, bronze stems set with gray leaves.

Size H: 10 in.; S: 15 in.

Spurge see *Euphorbia*

Stachys byzantina
(Lamb's ears)

Lamb's lugs, bunny ears, lamb's tongue—the number of popular names indicates that everyone knows this plant. This is not surprising for its soft, felt-like leaves are distinctive and it is easy to grow, spreading rapidly into gray carpets. The mauve-pink flowers emerge from white woolly buds in midsummer. As the flower spikes mature, the basal leaves deteriorate but the appearance of the plant improves once the flowers have been removed. Even with this treatment, lamb's ears should be dug up every other year and the best pieces replanted. The cultivar 'Silver Carpet' flowers only occasionally and is better for ground cover.

Size H: 1½ ft.; S: 1 ft. **Planting partner** *Rosa rugosa* 'Roseraie de l'Hay.'

Stonecrop see *Sedum*

Sun rose see *Helianthemum*

Thymus
(Thyme)

There are many thymes, all of which are suitable for growing on dry soils and are good on alkaline soils.

Planting partner *Helictotrichon sempervirens*.

T. praecox is a truly flat carpeter, creeping and rooting to cover quite a large area in time. Clusters of tiny

Sedum 'Ruby Glow'

flowers in purple, pink, white or crimson smother the plants in summer.

Size H: ½ in.

T. pseudolanuginosus makes rapid and dense cover, its woolly, gray leaves almost hiding the pink flowers which are produced in late summer.

Size H: ⅝ in.

The following thymes all make neat little evergreen bushes:

T. vulgaris, the common thyme, is the indispensable herb that is used in cooking. There are good variegated forms including 'Silver Posie.'

Size H: 8 in.; S: 1 ft.

T. × citriodorus 'Aureus', the golden lemon thyme, has lilac flowers which are carried in summer.

Size H: 4 in.; S: 10 in.

T. praecox 'Porlock' is a strong grower with mauve-pink flowers produced in early summer.

Size H and S: 1 ft.

Yarrow see *Achillea*

Index

Page numbers in *italics* refer to illustrations; numbers in **bold** to the chapter "Key plants."

Abelia 110
  A. × grandiflora 27, 71 (6–9)
  A. 'Kentish Belle' 72 (8–10)
  A. schumannii 71 (7–9)
Abutilon 72
  A. megapotamicum 72 (8–10)
  A. vitifolium 12, 71–2 (8–10)
Acacia
  A. dealbata 72 (9–11)
  A. retinodes 72 (9–11)
Acaena adscendens 88 (5–8)
Acanthus see Bear's breeches
Acer see Maple
Achillea see Yarrow
Acid soils 34
Adonis annua 25 (annual)
Aesculus californica 63 (7–9)
Agapanthus 16, *17*, 55, *55*, 83
Agrostemma githago 25 (annual)
Ailanthus altissima see Tree of Heaven
Albizia julibrissin see Silk tree
Alchemilla 54, *77*, *93*
  A. mollis 102 (4–7)
Alfalfa 38
Alkaline soils 35
Allium
  A. aflatunense 45 (4–8)
  A. caeruleum 95 (4–9)
  A. cernuum 95 (4–9)
  A. christophii 95 (4–9)
  A. karataviense 95 (5–9)
  A. siculum 95 (4–9)
Aloe 30
Aloysia triphylla see Lemon verbena
Alpine snow gum (*Eucalyptus pauciflora niphophila*) 62 (8–10)
  E. gunnii 86 (9–10)
Alyssum 12, 79
Amaryllis belladonna 27 (7–10)
Anemone
  A. blanda 95 (5–8)
  A. hupehensis 101 (4–8)
Annuals 94, 100, 101, 104
Anthemis
  A. punctata cupaniana 77, **118** (5–9)
  A. tinctoria **118** (4–8)
Apple *see* Crab apple
Aralia elata see Japanese angelica tree
Arbutus unedo see Strawberry tree
Arctostaphylos see Bearberry
Arizona ash (*Fraxinus velutina*) 60 (7–9)
Armeria see Thrift
Artemisia 38, 57, *58*, 77, **118–19**
  A. alba **119** (5–9)
  A. absinthium 57, *89* (5–8)

A. arborescens 71 5–9)
A. dracunculus see Tarragon
A. ludoviciana 84, *91* (4–8)
A. 'Powis Castle' *58* (8–10)
A. stelleriana 53, *58* (3–8)
Arum
  A. italicum italicum 74 (6–9)
  A. italicum marmoratum 37 (6–9)
Ash (*Fraxinus*) 22, 60
Asphodeline 99
Aster see Michaelmas daisy
Atriplex halimus 65, *88* (7–9)
Aucuba japonica 66, 67, *75* (7–9)
Aurinia saxatilis 88 (4–7)
Azalea 12
Azara microphylla 101 (7–10)

Ballota pseudodictamnus 77, *96* (7–9)
Banks 17–18, 20–3
  see also Slopes
Baptisia australis 91 (4–9)
Bark chippings 29
Bark mulch 42
Bay *see* Sweet bay
Beans, winter 38
Bearberry (*Arctostaphylos*) 12
  A. uva-ursi 77 (3–7)
Bearded iris 99
Bear's breeches (*Acanthus*) 16, 83, **118**
  A. mollis latifolius **118** (6–9)
  A. spinosus **118** (6–9)
Beauty bush (*Kolkwitzia amabilis*) 92, *96* (5–9)
Bedding plants 11, *24*
Berberis 12, *63*, 65, 66, 68, *97*, 104
  B. darwinii 66 (7–9)
  B. gagnepainii 68 (7–9)
  B. × media 68 (6–9)
  B. stenophylla 57, 66 (6–9)
  B. temolaica 88 (6–9)
  B. thunbergii 25, 65, 68, *84*, *87*, *87*, *88*, *96* (5–8)
  B. verruculosa 68 (6–9)
  B. wilsoniae 68, 83 (6–9)
Bergenia 30, *75*, 76
  B. cordifolia 79, 83 (4–8)
  B. 'Sunningdale' *75* (4–8)
Berries
  Berberis 97, 104
  Cotoneaster 63, 104
  holly 63, 64
Betula see Birch
Bidens ferulifolia 94 (9–10)
Biennials 94
Birch (*Betula*) 23
  B. albosinensis 28, 62 (5–7)
  B. ermanii 60, 62 (5–7)
  B. jacquemontii 62 (5–7)
  Swedish (*B. pendula*) 20, 62 (3–6)
Black locust (*Robinia pseudoacacia*) 60 (4–9)
Borders 96–7

Boston ivy (*Parthenocissus tricuspidata*) 73 (5–8)
Box (*Buxus*) 15, 22, 24, 25, 45, 51, 63
  B. microphylla koreana 79 (5–8)
  common (*B. sempervirens*) 63, 64, 76, 79 (6–8)
  hedges 64, 65
Box acacia (*Robinia hispida*) 26, 72 (6–8)
Brachyglottis 45, 69, 110 (9–10)
Briza media 83 (4–8)
Bronze fennel (*Foeniculum vulgare*) 88 (4–9)
Broom (*Cytisus*) 12, 17, 21, 55, **112**, **113**
  C. battandieri 72, *96* (8–9)
  C. × praecox 34 (7–9)
  C. scoparius 23 (6–8)
  C. 'Zeelandia' 21 (7–9)
Broom (*Genista*)
  G. aetnensis 81, **113** (9–10)
Broom, Spanish (*Spartium junceum*) *58*, **117** (8–10)
Brunnera macrophylla 75, 79 (4–8)
Buddleia 92, **110**
  B. alternifolia 81 (5–9)
  B. auriculata 72 (8–9)
  B. colvilei 72 (8–9)
  B. crispa 72 (5–9)
  B. davidii 72 (5–9)
  B. fallowiana alba 72, *89* (8–9)

B. 'Lochinch' 110 (6–9)
B. 'Pink Delight' 92 (5–9)
Bulbs 30, 40, 74, 95
Bupleurum fruticosum 58 (7–10)
Buxus see Box

Cacti 30
Calamintha nepeta 76 (6–8)
Calandrinia 57
Calcifuges 35
Calendula officinalis see Marigold
Californian poppy (*Eschscholzia*) 56, 103 (annual)
Californian tree poppy (*Romneya coulteri*) 12, 55, 57, **115** (7–10)
Californian wild lilac (*Ceanothus*) 17, 20, *27*, 69, 70–1, **110–11**
  C. arboreus 71 (9–10)
  C. 'Blue Mound' 69 (8–10)
  C. 'Burkwoodii' *27* (8–10)
  C. 'Cascade' 111 (8–10)
  C. × delileanus 92, *96*, **111** (6–9)
  C. impressus 72 (8–10)
  C. thyrsiflorus repens 20, 69, 71 (8–10)
Callistemon salignus 71, 72 (9–11)
Calluna vulgaris see Scotch heather
Campanula
  C. persicifolia 33 (3–8)

C. rotundifolia 25 (3–8)
Campsis 16
  C. radicans flava 73 (5–9)
  C. × tagliabuana 73 (6–9)
Candytuft (*Iberis sempervirens*) 78 (4–8)
Caragana arborescens 63 (2–7)
Cardoon (*Cynara cardunculus*) 82, 84, *89*, **120** (6–8)
Carpenteria californica 72 (8–9)
Carpinus betulus see Hornbeam
Caryopteris × clandonensis 53 (5–9)
Castanea sativa 63 (5–7)
Catalpa
  C. bignonioides 82 (5–9)
  C. speciosa 82 (5–9)
Catmint (*Nepeta*) 7, 21, 77, 78, *79*, **122**
  N. × faassenii **122** (4–9)
  N. × 'Six Hills Giant' **122** (4–9)
Ceanothus see Californian wild lilac
Cedar (*Cedrus*) 61
Celastrus scandens 73 (3–8)
Centaurea see Knapweed
Centranthus see Valerian
Cerastium see Snow-in-summer
Ceratostigma see Plumbago
Cercis siliquastrum see Judas tree
Chaenomeles 70, 73
  C. × superba 74 (5–9)
Chamaemelum nobile 77 (6–9)

Plant hardiness zones

This hardiness map will help you to establish which plants are most suitable for your garden. **The zones 1–11 are based on the average annual minimum temperature for each zone and appear after the plant entry in the index.** The lower number indicates the northernmost zone in which the plant can survive the winter and the higher number the most southerly area in which it will perform consistently.

ZONE 1	BELOW −50° F
ZONE 2	−50° TO −40°
ZONE 3	−40° TO −30°
ZONE 4	−30° TO −20°
ZONE 5	−20° TO −10°
ZONE 6	−10° TO 0°
ZONE 7	0° TO 10°
ZONE 8	10° TO 20°
ZONE 9	20° TO 30°
ZONE 10	30° TO 40°
ZONE 11	ABOVE 40°

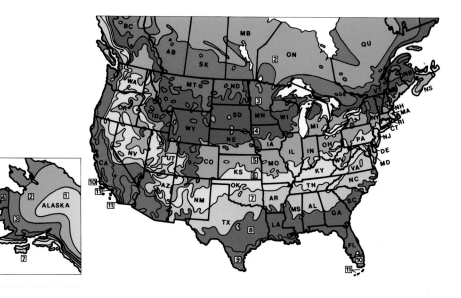

Acknowledgments

Author's acknowledgments

To Susanne Mitchell of the RHS and Jane O'Shea of Conran Octopus go my thanks for inviting me to write about the dry garden and for their encouragement and patience. I am grateful to Alison Dove, Jean Day, Diane Mann, Brian Humphreys, Pamela Harper and Jean Melville Clark for their assistance or advice. Lastly, my thanks go to my publisher's staff, especially Helen Ridge and Lesley Craig, whose skill and constant good humor made the editing process so enjoyable.

Publisher's acknowledgments

The publisher would like to thank the following photographers and organizations for their kind permission to reproduce the photographs in this book:

1 Trevor Wood/Robert Harding Picture Library; 2–3 Clive Boursnell (Denton Hall); 4–5 Clive Nichols (Hadspen Gardens, Somerset); 6–7 Juliette Wade (Fulford Farm, Northamptonshire); 8 Michael Busselle; 9 left Jacqui Hurst/Country Living; 9 right Andre W. Brown/A–Z Botanical; 10 Jerry Harpur (designer: Simon Hopkinson/ Hollington Nursery, Berkshire); 11 Jerry Harpur (designer: Christopher Masson); 12 Jerry Harpur (The Beth Chatto Gardens); 13 Brigitte Thomas; 14–15 Jerry Harpur (La Casella, Claus Scheinert); 16 Vincent Motte; 17 Jerry Harpur (La Casella, Claus Scheinert); 18 Jerry Harpur (Stellenberg, The Cape); 19 Brigitte Thomas; 22 Georges Lévêque; 23 Jerry Harpur (Churchill Campania, Tasmania); 24 Jerry Harpur (designer: Bruce Kelly, N.Y.); 25 Jacqui Hurst/Country Living (Mark Rumary's garden); 28 Elizabeth Whiting & Associates; 29 John Fielding; 30 left Georges Lévêque; 30 right Georges Lévêque; 32–3 Clive Nichols (Mottisfont Abbey, Hampshire); 35 left Georges Lévêque (Keukenhof, Holland); 35 right John Fielding; 37 above Noel Kavanagh; 37 below Jane Legate/Garden Picture Library; 38 Marianne Majerus; 39 Boys Syndication; 40 Jerry Harpur (The Beth Chatto Gardens); 41 left Jerry Harpur (The Beth Chatto Gardens); 41 right Mike Mackrill/A–Z Botanical; 43 above Jerry Harpur; 43 below John Glover; 45 Clive Nichols (Barnsley House Garden, Gloucester); 47 Harry Smith Collection; 48 J.C. Mayer/Le Scanff/Garden Picture Library; 51 Jerry Harpur (La Casella, France); 52–3 Jerry Harpur (The Beth Chatto Gardens); 54 Hugh Palmer/Homes and Garden/Robert Harding Syndication (Saltwood Castle); 55 Jerry Harpur; 56 Brian Carter/ Garden Picture Library; 57 Didier Willery/Garden Picture Library; 60 John Glover/Garden Picture Library (Coates Manor, Sussex); 61 Brigitte Thomas/Garden Picture Library; 62 Hugh Palmer (Newby Hall); 63 Elizabeth Whiting & Associates; 64 John Glover/Garden Picture Library; 65 Jerry Harpur (designer: Tania Young, Perth); 66 Georges Lévêque; 67 left A–Z Botanical; 67 right Zig Leszczynski/Oxford Scientific Films; 68 John Glover/ Garden Picture Library (Valley Gardens, Windsor); 70 Christian Sarramon; 71 Marianne Majerus; 72 Andrew Lawson; 73 John Glover; 77 below Elizabeth Whiting & Associates; 78 Christine Ternynck; 79 Brigitte Thomas/ Garden Picture Library; 80 Jerry Harpur (Denmans, Sussex); 81 Tania Midgley; 82 Clive Nichols (Copton Ash, Kent); 83 Michèle Lamontagne; 84 Elizabeth Whiting & Associates; 85 left Brigitte Thomas (Sissinghurst Castle, Kent); 85 right Eric Crichton; 86 Neil Campbell-Sharp (Tintinhull); 87 Tania Midgley (Brook Cottage); 90–1 Tania Midgley; 92 Jerry Harpur (The Beth Chatto Gardens); 93 Clive Nichols (Glazeley Old Rectory, Shropshire); 94 Clive Nichols (Red Gables, Worcestershire); 95 Clive Nichols (The Beth Chatto Gardens); 98–9 Noel Kavanagh (Turn End, Buckinghamshire); 100 Marianne Majerus; 101 J. Elliotts/John Fielding; 102 Marianne Majerus; 103 Elizabeth Whiting & Associates; 104 Jerry Harpur (The Dingle, Welshpool); 105 Jerry Harpur (Hatfield House); 106–7 Neil Campbell-Sharp; 110 Insight; 112 John Glover/Garden Picture Library; 113 Dan Sams/A–Z Botanical; 114–15 Photos Horticultural; 116 John Glover; 117 Anthony Cooper/A–Z Botanical; 118 Michèle Lamontagne/ Garden Picture Library; 120 Brian Carter/Garden Picture Library; 121 Clive Nichols (East Lambrook Manor); 122 Clive Nichols; 123 Andrew Lawson.

The publisher also thanks: Jackie Matthews, Barbara Nash and Janet Smy.

Index compiled by Indexing Specialists, Hove, East Sussex BN3 2DJ.